The Milan Approach to
Family Therapy

The Milan Approach to Family Therapy

Guido L. Burbatti, M.D.
Laura Formenti

Translated by Elena Cosmo

Jason Aronson Inc.
Northvale, New Jersey
London

Library of Congress Cataloging-in-Publication Data

Burbatti, Guido.
    The Milan approach to family therapy.

    Translations of: La famiglia e il suo
modello.
    Includes bibliographies and index.
    1. Family psychotherapy.   2. Family
psychotherapy—Italy—Milan.   I. Formenti,
Laura.   II. Title.   [DNLM: 1. Family Therapy
—methods.   2. Models, Psychological.
WM 430.5.F2 B946m]
RC488.5.B7813   1988   616.89′156   87-19595
ISBN 0-87668-972-1

CONTENTS

PREFACE

This study has just been published in Milan. The authors are part of the Milan group of family therapy. The Milan school's approach to dealing with family disorders has achieved international renown not only on the Continent—Italy, France, and Germany—but also in the United States. Their work is discussed in some detail by such leading figures of the systemic school as Lynn Hoffman in her book *Foundations of Family Therapy* (1981) and Bradford P. Keeney and Jeffrey M. Ross in the recently published *Mind in Therapy: Constructing Systemic Family Therapies* (1985).

The Milan school is one branch of a larger movement within modern psychiatry that is seeking to apply the methods and insights of cybernetics to the analysis and treatment of behavioral disorders. This approach is inspired by the work of Gregory Bateson and is an application of Bateson's theories about communication to the treatment of mentally ill patients.

The book is divided into five chapters. The first presents a clear and concise exposition of the theoretical framework; the subsequent four chapters describe the different phases of therapy as it proceeds from the moment a family calls to the family's dismissal from therapy: hypothesization, conduct of the session, interventions, evaluation of the results. At the end of each chapter, its theoretical contents are illustrated by the verbatim transcript (with running commentary) of selected parts of a true case history. This provides an illustration of the authors' working method.

This work is the first comprehensive attempt to lay before the public a full, systematic exposition of the theory and the techniques particular to the Milan approach, as applied during the authors' clinical work with families. The work is designed for those familiar with the systemic model who are interested in learning about a conceptual approach now universally acknowledged as one of the most rigorous and complex lines of thought, both from a theoretical viewpoint and from its relevance to clinical practice.

THE
SYSTEMIC MODEL
Chapter 1 | # IN FAMILY THERAPY

This chapter presents an introduction to the model on which our work is based. It is important in a book that intends to be a quasi manual to provide an explicit model and an introduction to the epistemological, theoretical, and methodological principles permeating all of our work. The model should:

Mark the unit of observation and analysis and the conceptual framework of reference. The descriptive nature of this work demands the adoption of a framework that gives an order to the mass of information provided by an event—in our case, a therapy. Therapeutic activity often requires a simplification of reality as a preliminary condition for effective intervention.

Introduce a terminology. Considering the confusion that reigns in clinical psychology and psychiatry, a single vocabulary common to all psychotherapists is impossible; at best, one can adopt a specific jargon related to the underlying model. Even so, the possibility remains that the same event will be interpreted differently by different therapists.

Set up limits. Adopting a specific model means not only opening up to possibilities otherwise precluded, but also eliminating others. Every form of therapy has its own limits: There are no interventions valid on all occasions nor interpretations that are always true.

Clarify the relationship between theory and practice. Models can carry out numerous functions. The one we will illustrate is an analogical model, one that is more applied than theoretical. It enables the transfer of theoretical concepts into therapeutic practice (Hesse 1966). The demand for intervention in a complex, sometimes unlivable climate, with ever bigger and more urgent problems, creates a situation in which the danger of falling into excessive instrumentalism is great. Therapists are often urged to consider first and foremost the effectiveness of their work, with little or no opportunity to evaluate what an effective therapy really is. As a matter of fact, practice is inextricably tied to the process through which problems are conceptualized. For this reason, in order to intervene effectively it becomes necessary, first of all, to agree on a definition for the term *therapy*—in other words, to adopt a model.

Thus we have decided to abandon the myth of objectivity, refusing every eclecticism and searching for methodological rigor and coherence.

FAMILY THERAPY

Family therapy is a form of psychotherapeutic intervention, based on communication and conversation, whose object is not the individual, as in the more classical forms of psychotherapy, but rather a social group.

However, if we try to deepen our knowledge of what is really meant by bringing a family into therapy, we encounter the first difficulties: Despite the apparently simple (or simplistic) definition of family therapy, a family cannot be accurately and objectively circumscribed. Case studies show the most disparate family typologies—from the patriarchal family, where three generations live together under one roof; to the restricted nucleus of a married couple with children, who may or may not be close to their respective families; to childless couples; separated families; cohabitants; friendships stronger than family ties themselves; and so on. These observations should point out the difficulty of establishing a precise criterion with regard to who constitutes the family to be taken into therapy. It is also clear that even if, in view of the need for order and continuity, our therapeutic processes almost invariably begin by meeting with the patient's cohabitants, in subsequent interviews a wider or different group may be included, if this is deemed useful to the therapy.

In reality, the problem is even bigger and involves the very definition of a family as a system, a definition that is fundamental to our work and that calls for a few explanations.

Family therapy does not identify itself entirely with our method, but rather embraces a vast number of heterogeneous techniques and theories, to the point that a family therapy movement, a community of therapists and scholars who use the same methods and terminology, does not exist. In the vast literature on family therapy,

Hoffman (1981) identified at least five different approaches, which she called historical, ecological, structural, strategic, and systemic. (For an exhaustive analysis of the theoretical and technical characteristics of each school, the reader can consult Hoffman's book, with its rich bibliography.)

In the therapeutic field, the origins of this active interest in the family can be traced back to the 1950s, when a few independent therapists almost secretly began including patients' families in the sessions. Initially, this approach was motivated by a need to gather information, but soon the observers were able to notice a connection between what the patient did and said (the so-called symptoms) and the modes of the family interactions. However, these were single, isolated incidents that were kept secret from the scientific community, and we can agree with Hoffman that there was no founder of family therapy, and no "first" family therapy interview (1981). This movement can thus be labeled only *a posteriori*, considering the deep differences that characterized it from the start. Actually, the different approaches to family therapy that have developed from that initial period have little in common, apart from having adopted the family as the subject for study and intervention.

Our approach, using Hoffman's classification, could be described, at least partially, as systemic. We emphasize its ties with an important research movement that has developed in the last 30 years alongside the therapeutic activity, which we call a model based on complexity in order to highlight its antisimplistic and anticausative epistemological connotations.

A MODEL BASED ON COMPLEXITY

The theoretical and epistemological premises underlying our working method have their roots in the general system theory developed by von Bertalanffy (1967, 1969) and in the "pattern which connects" conceptualized by Bateson (1972, 1979).

General system theory is an integrated and interdisciplinary holistic approach to the most disparate fields of human knowledge. It is based on the concept of system, namely of an organized unit determined by the reciprocal interaction of its components. The distinguishing feature of a system is totality: The whole is greater than the sum of its parts.

It is a general theory, above single disciplines. Its application in our field has prompted the characterization of families as systems exchanging material, energy, and information with the environment—in other words, open systems. The identification of the patients' families as systems, especially in those cases with a psychiatric diagnosis, has made possible the development of new psychotherapeutic intervention techniques. These observations emphasize that the transposition of concepts and theories has had eminently practical effects: The requirements of therapy have imposed adjustments and simplifications to the original theory.

Another important contribution to our approach comes from the work of Bateson, the anthropologist and cybernetician who founded the research group on human and animal communication known as the "Bateson project" in Palo Alto, California (Bateson 1972, Sluzki and Ransom 1976).

Bateson's interest in the pattern which connects (1979) arose from cybernetics, a science founded in the 1940s by Wiener (1965). Wiener proposed to revolutionize the scientific world by diverting scientific attention from the study of quantity, causes, and substances—typical of classical physics and of the disciplines inspired by it—to the study of relations, organizations, and form. The general principle of cybernetics was, and is, that of information.

If we examine the history of the Palo Alto group—which included researchers in different disciplines who worked first on the Bateson project in the 1950s and the 1960s and then on the Mental Research Institute project (Watzlawick and Weakland 1977)—we become aware that two main approaches and traditions merged here. There is the theoretical background and research work of the Bateson group. For many years, this group studied the characteristics of communication processes in different contexts (play, learning, humor, and so on), and only at a later date did it deal with schizophrenic communication, in particular with the use of signals that identify the modes of communication (Bateson 1972, Bateson et al. 1956). A second contribution came when Jackson joined the group as a clinical consultant. Since Bateson's research was for the most part anthropological in nature, the interference of the observer with the object of the study was limited as much as possible, unlike psychotherapy. But the confluence of the hypotheses on communication and the first therapeutic experiences with schizophrenics and their families gave life to one of the most discussed etiopathological models in the last 30 years: the double bind theory.

This theory took shape with the discovery of a pattern, a model of communication, observed every time the person diagnosed as schizophrenic was watched in interaction with other family members (Sluzki and Ransom 1976). According to the double bind hypothesis, schizophrenic behavior consists of a message that acquires meaning within a no-way-out situation, and precisely in a situation where family relationships have never been clearly defined. The effect of the symptomatic behaviors would be to avoid the metacommunication between the patient and the rest of the family.

In 1956 Bateson and associates described this pattern for

the first time (Bateson et al. 1956), adopting a dyadic scheme in which two people were involved—for example, a patient and the patient's mother. Afterward, the formulation of the theory was further circularized and became triadic, and thus more in accordance with the complexity of human interaction (Weakland 1960). In recent times researchers have almost completely abandoned this theory, although it is used by clinicians in view of its practical relevance.

Jackson (1957) also formulated the family homeostasis hypothesis, another mainstay of our model. This hypothesis derives from the observation of the frequent clashes between the psychotherapeutic practice on a single individual and those behaviors inside the patient's family that seem to have an inhibitory effect on change, such as the appearance of symptoms in the sane family members following an improvement in the sick member (Jackson and Weakland 1961).

The family is organized as a dynamic system with a stable structure. The behavior and interactions of the various members, the indication of one of them as sick and the request for therapy would be such as to maintain the status quo and correct the changes introduced by the therapists or others through a mechanism of negative feedback (Watzlawick et al. 1967).

It was Jackson, following these observations, who introduced conjoint family therapy, a type of therapy that involved interviews with all family members. Jackson considered it a form of homeopathic therapy: It was based on the idea that the particular communicatory mechanisms used by family members may be used against them for therapeutic purposes, according to the homeopathic concept of *similia similibus curantur*.

The interest in the paradoxes of communication, formulation of the double bind theory, Jackson's brilliant intuitions, to a great extent led directly to the various techniques of paradoxical intervention (see Chapter 4) and what came to be called the strategic approach. As opposed to the traditional forms of intervention, the strategic approach has been structured from the beginning as a brief therapy (Weakland et al. 1974), with a small number of sessions and a long time lapse between them. Furthermore, it is structured as a problem-oriented therapy, and thus a behavior-oriented one, within the system that directly or indirectly sustains it (Haley 1976, Watzlawick et al. 1974), as well as a relational therapy since it is based more on the mathematical concept of relation or function than on the concept of content (Haley 1963, Watzlawick et al. 1967). As clinicians and theoreticians, we owe a great deal to Haley, Watzlawick, Weakland, and Sluzki. But there are undoubtedly differences between our methods and theirs; our approach—the systemic approach—places a greater emphasis on meanings and, consequently, on the Batesonian concept of world view. For a more complete comparison, we refer the reader to other works (Hoffman 1981, MacKinnon 1983).

The importance of the model based on complexity lies with the fact that it provides a new world view, a different and more complex way of viewing life and its problems. It refuses the classical rationality, founded on the search for causes, that permeates Newtonian determinism, because determinism is inadequate for a phenomenon such as life, which is not reducible to linear cause-and-effect relationships.

Today, the theories of von Bertalanffy and the research conducted by the Palo Alto school are probably partially outdated, but the conception of science underlying them is still of great interest, and numerous schools have arisen from these groups, giving life to submodels, specific theories, and different interventions, all with a link to that common philosophical root. In the therapeutic field, the model based on complexity has assumed different facets. We will limit ourselves, however, to describing our own work, which is quite specific and not representative of all that can be done within the model.

THE MILAN SCHOOL

We have referred to the systemic approach, characteristic of the Milan school, as our model of therapeutic intervention. When speaking of family therapy in Italy, one must mention the pioneer work conducted by a group of therapists operating in Milan under the guidance of Selvini Palazzoli since 1967, when, as she herself narrates, the adventure of the conceptual leap from a model based on energy to a model based on information was initially tackled (Selvini Palazzoli et al. 1978). The original group—which included Selvini Palazzoli, Boscolo,Cecchin, and Prata—worked together for some ten years, developing a therapeutic model based on a family system approach to replace the individual/psychodynamic one, thus creating a form unique and profitable enough, from a theoretical and practical point of view, to be considered a school of its own. The international fame of the Milan group's work has contributed to the creation of a new generation of therapists and social workers trained in accordance with the systemic approach, known as the Milan school. They are currently working in the most disparate contexts, from the public service sector to the centers for family therapy. Among these, unique in its own right, is the Centro per lo Studio e la Terapia della Famiglia at Niguarda Hospital, which combines clinical practice with research and training activities, the latter in cooperation with the Gregory Bateson Center.

A systematic description of the therapeutic techniques used by the Selvini Palazzoli group dates back to 1975, when the book *Paradox and Counterparadox* was published (Selvini Palazzoli et al. 1978). In this work, the Milan group applied to therapeutic practice a few theoretical concepts formulated in *Pragmatics of Human Communication* (Watzlawick et al. 1967), the manifesto of the Palo Alto group and basic reading for all family therapists.

On the basis of the concept of therapeutic paradox (Bateson et al. 1956, Hoffman 1981, Sluzki and Ransom 1976, Watzlawick et al. 1967, 1974, Weeks and L'Abate 1982), derived from the double bind hypothesis and the concept of homeopathic therapy (Watzlawick et al. 1967), the Milan therapists elaborated the counterparadox, a set of intervention techniques that had a paradoxical pragmatic effect on families, in order to beat them on their own turf. The counterparadox, in a ritual or prescriptive form, or simply as a positive connotation (see Chapter 4), seemed to work particularly well with those families with a highly confused and disturbed style of communication— for example, families of anorexic patients, of which the group has ample case studies.

THE SYSTEMIC APPROACH TO FAMILY THERAPY

The concepts set forth here represent a general outline of family therapy. They will be illustrated starting with the very general and basic concepts and moving to the more specific and technical ones. Such an expository structure has been chosen to reflect the simple and linear structure of the language rather than the idea, alien to us, of a simple derivative (deductive) relationship from the general hypotheses to the more specific ones. We feel that practice is not only a means of verification, but also a medium whereby theory is elaborated. This means that the relationship between the two elements of the science-making process—if two distinct elements can be envisaged—must be circular. As Bateson (1972) has pointed out, between observations and fundamentals "you must achieve a sort of pincers maneuver" (p. xxi).

THE FAMILY AS AN OBJECT OF ANALYSIS AND INTERVENTION

The primary hypothesis of the Milan approach to family therapy, as stated in *Paradox and Counterparadox* (Selvini Palazzoli et al. 1978), concerns the choice of the family unit as the object of analysis and intervention. *The family is a self-correcting system that governs itself through rules established over a period of time by trial and error.*

This definition of family is connected with such concepts as *system*, *rule*, and *learning through trial and error*, which could themselves occupy entire chapters in view of their complexity and the need to refer to different authors and periods. We shall limit ourselves to a brief description.

It has been said that family therapy regards the family as a *system*, borrowing this concept from a range of disciplines. According to the classic definition of Hall and Fagen, a system is a "set of objects and relations between the objects and their attributes" (1956). Alternatively, one may adopt the definition proposed by von Bertalanffy, the author of *General System Theory*: A system is a set of elements that interact (1969). The latter definition stresses the reciprocity of the relationships within the system. From a more communication-oriented point of view, using the words of Keeney, a cybernetician of the new generation, a system can be defined as "a cybernetic network that processes information" (1979, p. 119). More exhaustive information concerning systems is provided by the great number of books dealing with this subject, both from a metadisciplinary (Bertalanffy 1969, Haire 1959, Miller 1965a,b,c) and a more specific (Buckley 1967, 1968, Gray et al. 1969) point of view. Of paramount importance is that the principal distinction for systems revolves around the interdependence of the input-output relations in the system–environment unit. In fact, if it is true that the various elements of a system are mutually interrelated, it is also true that a system exists in a certain environment and is determinable and determines itself on the basis of the exchanges of information with this setting. As can be deduced, a system is not something real, but rather the outcome of a choice the observer makes on the basis of several elements, and as such it is a description, a linguistic act. Consequently, any determinable network that processes information—from a cell to an individual to society as a whole—may represent the more appropriate object for analysis in relation to a specific problem.

Choosing the family as a unit of intervention does not mean that it is really a system, nor that it is the only system that can be taken into consideration. By defining it as such, we are not making any assumption. We do not want to identify *tout court* the systemic approach to psychotherapy with family therapy. Therefore, the selection of the family as a unit of intervention is useful: This is the system most readily available for therapy and the one in which people live most of their lives. Intervention in this system, rather than in others (school, work, peer group, and so on) can be particularly effective.

The family is a rule-governed system. This concept was introduced by Jackson (1965a,b) to refer to those redundancies or interactional models that characterize family communication to the point that it is possible to recognize recurrent patterns within members' interactions. According to this hypothesis, every family has its own interactional rules. As defined by Jackson, a rule is a "pattern imposed by the observer on the significant redundancies of marital interaction, and should always be understood metaphorically, with the tacit preface, 'It seems as if. . . .' " (Jackson 1965a, p. 592). Such a metaphorical use of the concept of rule would be "desirable as long as we avoid the pitfalls of reification and acknowledge the fictitious nature of all our constructs" (p. 593). Thus, rules are to be viewed within an epistemology of complexity, from a nonrealistic point of view, as Bateson stressed when citing Korzybski: "The map is not the territory" (Bateson 1970, p. 449). Every theoretical formulation shows traces of choices made *a priori* and never coincides with reality. Since misunderstandings can arise in this respect, in more recent times the concept of rule has been harshly criticized (Dell 1980b, 1982). In its place, preference is now given to alternative terms, more clearly stressing the active role of the observer—in this case the therapist—in the construction of interpretative models.

Another concept is that of *learning through trial and error*. The use of this concept, historically derived from research on animal learning and conditioning, concerns us, especially in relation to its proximity to the concept of adaptation. Bateson made an enormous contribution to the study of the process of learning by applying to these phenomena the Russellian theory of logical types. In his essay "The Logical Categories of Learning and Communication" (1964), Bateson ascribes to living organisms the prerogative of learning through trial and error, since they can make wrong choices: "These wrong choices are appropriately called 'error' when they are of such a kind that they would provide information to the organism which might contribute to his future skill" (p. 286). Bateson defines two different levels of learning, in relation to the error committed and the organism's consequent correction. At the first level (Learning I), the animal must take a different course of action while remaining within the behavioral context of the "wrong choice." That which is required at the second level (Learning II) is a shift to a different set of alternatives; what is modified is the marked context.

A characteristic common to all families who enter therapy seems to be precisely this inability to change the set of alternatives, leading to a "game without end" (Bateson 1972, Watzlawick et al. 1967, 1974).

THE ETIOPATHOLOGICAL HYPOTHESIS

As far as psychopathology in particular is concerned, the fundamental hypothesis underlying our work is directly connected to the preceding one: Symptoms are part of a significant interaction between the members of a system. They are a communicatory behavior, like all the behaviors taking place in the family.

What differentiates this approach from the more traditional ones is the attribution of a specific meaning to the symptom dependent on the communicatory context in which the symptom manifests itself, and consequently dependent on family rules rather than on the individual psychology of the symptomatic member.

Another interesting aspect of this hypothesis is its neutrality toward pathology. Since the behaviors of the members of a system are the product of reciprocal interaction—as we have established when defining the concept of family—even a symptom that might appear absurd and incomprehensible to a stranger proves functional to the nonsymptomatic actions of the sane members when examined within the context of the family communicatory patterns. Hence the use of the term *identified patient* to highlight the complex process underlying the definition of patient, which often makes it impossible to foresee which member of a system will become the "sick" one. The determination of a pathological behavior and the subsequent diagnostic labeling also follow tortuous paths, involving institutions outside the family. But as soon as a systemic view is adopted, one no longer deals with a symptomatic individual but rather with a symptomatic system, a system comprising the symptom as one of its usual communication modes and presumably utilizing it within its own working mechanisms and organizations (Bateson et al. 1956, Selvini Palazzoli et al. 1978).

THEORY OF CHANGE
AND THE PURPOSE OF THERAPY

It is necessary to establish what we mean by therapy. From a communication-oriented point of view, therapeutic intervention aims at the improvement of the patient's communication system through a particular use of communication (Ruesch and Bateson 1951). In our approach the disappearance of a symptom is somehow related to a change occurring in the family game that has made the symptom unnecessary (Watzlawick et al. 1967). From a more practical point of view, this means that the primary goal of therapy is not a change in the behaviors and thoughts of the single individual, but in the structure of meanings, relationships, and rules in the system as a whole. Therapeutic intervention is based on a direct or indirect redefinition of the contextual framework in which the nonadaptive behaviors take place; in other words, the family is placed in a condition in which it can experience new situations or give alternative interpretations to the same situation. The redefinition thus performed unveils the family game, making it impractical. Such a holistic approach, unlike the outdated "schizophrenogenic mother" theory and other similar approaches, and even the first double bind theory, avoids focusing on the identified patient as well as on any other single family member. In fact, according to the cybernetics of self, no one has the power to rule the family system but the system itself (Bateson 1971).

METHODOLOGICAL OUTLINE

The premises underlying the model based on complexity also influence the methodological choices, the structuring of the therapeutic setting, and the selection of therapeutic techniques. We are referring to the Batesonian observations about the context as a "matrix of meaning" (Bateson 1972). According to this view therapy is ultimately a skillful use of context markers, as Bateson defines those "signals whose major function is to *classify* contexts" (Bateson 1964, p. 289). In family therapy, the most striking context markers are those provided by the participation in the sessions of all family members, by the fact that the therapist asks a certain type of question and by the presence of a supervisor behind the one-way screen. When used jointly with comments and situations specific to the system, the context markers make it possible to rapidly define the relationship between the family and the therapist.

The use of "punctuations" (different or even antithetic interpretations of family problems) during sessions is a restructuring technique based on the hypothesis that different modes of codification of events are related to differences in the underlying premises. Hence we respect each and every punctuation provided by the family.

At this point, it should be clear that every element of

therapy and every solution adopted has a definite link with the underlying theoretical model and is justified by it. This implies that, at least on an ideal plane, the therapists working together on a case know what they are doing at every moment, and are thus able to reconstruct and explain their intervention strategies.

TEAMWORK

A fundamental feature that distinguishes our model is the emphasis constantly placed on the team as a whole rather than on individual therapists. To make possible a cybernetic, namely a circular, work method, it is necessary for the team to become a mind. In a Batesonian sense, a mind is a system that gathers and processes information and elaborates an output of some sort (Bateson 1979). Every message given to the family is a product of this mind, and thus of the entire therapeutic system. In the sessions, the interviewer is joined by at least one other therapist who supervises the interview behind a one-way screen. Moreover, the supervisor and the other team members take an active part in the discussions preceding and following the session. The information acquired is elaborated on, and the most important decisions are made. This work method avoids the paradoxes of self-observation, always incumbent when the observer of a situation is also a part of it (by definition, the therapist participates in the interaction taking place during the session and, to a certain extent, after it). This method is also consistent with Bateson's thesis that the confrontation of multiple descriptions generates information on a new logical level. The therapeutic team is thus able to compare different perspectives of the problem and its possible solutions. Generally, these punctuations are linear, but their confrontation reveals how everything is connected in an increasingly complex and circular structure. Finally, teamwork introduces all the advantages of supervision (neutrality, didactic potential, an opportunity to correct the way the session is conducted, and so on). These are enhanced by the fact that, since the correction takes place immediately, it is more accurate and thus more helpful to the interviewer (and it generally creates positive expectations within the family).

The importance of teamwork is particularly evident during the pre- and postsession discussions. In the presession discussion every aspect of the problem is investigated in order to formulate hypotheses with regard to the functioning of the system. This includes the request for therapy: How did the family come to be in therapy? What do they expect? What relationship do they propose to the therapists? These hypotheses will also suggest a strategy for conducting the session, a few topics for further investigation, and the information to be sought or introduced during the interview.

In the postsession discussion the initial hypotheses are reexamined, confirmed, or revised; an intervention is elaborated; and in some cases, its effects are predicted. During these discussions, linear hypotheses generate the systemic hypothesis, which is set on a higher logical level and does not belong to any single team member but rather comes from the team as a whole.

THE THREE PHASES OF THERAPY

Breaking up therapeutic activity into three distinct phases may appear reductive, since it does not do justice to the complexity of the therapeutic relationship or, above all, to the therapeutic process itself, which cannot be easily placed into static schemes. Furthermore, the therapeutic process can be divided into as many stages as there are possible segments of our experience—in other words, on the basis of an infinite number of schemes. Nevertheless, if the communicatory relationship established between the therapist and the family is regarded as the fundamental element of therapy, the whole family therapy process can be segmented into three phases: engagement, therapy, and dismissal. Naturally, each phase is influenced by the model adopted.

In a systemic-cybernetic approach to therapy the *engagement*, or the moment when the family is taken into therapy, is a crucial phase. The rules governing the therapeutic relationship, which usually will be enforced throughout the therapy, are negotiated more or less implicitly at this time. In addition, since our model attaches a great importance to communication, the therapist carefully takes note of how messages are given and received, of possible discrepancies, and of the specific difficulties of each family in accepting certain rules. During this first phase the therapist gives information regarding the context ("context markers"), establishes metarules, highlights the rights and obligations of the participants in the session, and claims certain prerogatives for himself. Finally, the therapist decides whether to take the family (system) into therapy or not.

After the first few sessions, certain aspects of the therapeutic relationship remain for which rules have not yet been established; the number of these aspects decreases as the communicatory interaction progresses. The family is "engaged" when it accepts the relationship proposed by the therapist—his rules and decisions concerning all the aspects of therapy, even the apparently trivial ones.

These are the minimal prerequisites for transition to the second stage, *therapy*, and they are by no means automatic. On the contrary, therapy is often slowed down by the threats to the therapeutic relationship imposed by the system or even by the impossibility of establishing this relationship. Failure of a member to attend a meeting, digressions from the subject or inaccurate answers to questions, attempts to impose one's own needs and demands when scheduling the sessions or even to influence the way the therapy is conducted, and to break apparently unimportant rules, can seriously undermine results. Each of these moves, in view of its homeostatic and thus antitherapeutic potential, calls for an accurate appraisal and an adequate countermove aimed at the reestablishment of the relationship so that its potential for change can be fully attained. The therapy is actually carried out by means of speeches and behaviors the team addresses to the family during the session. Each of these messages is linked to a systemic hypothesis formulated by the team on the basis of the available information. Thus, by "therapy" we mean both the conduct of the therapeutic interview and the intervention—for the most part paradoxical—that the team carries out at the end of the session.

The *dissolution of the therapeutic contract* is linked to the solution of the problem. This calls for careful consideration, since there are no set criteria for determining the exact moment in which the therapist's task is concluded, nor is it possible to establish whether it is the family or the therapist who should make this decision. In this type of therapy, more than in others, patients seldom feel any gratitude toward the therapist for their improvement, which they ascribe to fortuitous circumstances within the system or related to the passing of time. Given these complications, it is most difficult to evaluate with a certain degree of scientific accuracy the therapeutic process once it is concluded. There are situations that call for an interpretation of the available data, such as those cases where the system shows disappointment and dissatisfaction with the outcome of the therapy, in spite of the fact that the disappearance of the symptom is evident. Does this mean that some hidden problems still remain unsolved? Or does it depend on the degree of gradualness that characterizes a short-term therapy like ours?

Generally, these difficulties are ignored, since the disappearance of the symptoms is assumed as the relevant change indicator. Even this solution, however, leaves a large margin of doubt (see Chapter 5).

SUBDIVISION OF THE SESSION

If we agree that therapy can be divided into three phases, each session can be classified either as an "engagement" (usually the first or, at the latest, the second session), a "therapeutic," or a "dismissal" session. A different kind of subdivision is one that considers each session as a separate "therapeutic unit." In this respect, one can envisage different phases in which such a unit can be articulated, roughly corresponding to the different functions sessions perform. We have adopted a subdivision of the session into four different activities, providing a logical framework for the material illustrated in the following chapters and enabling us to highlight those aspects of our work we deem most interesting. Such a division appears to be the most suitable to the didactic purpose of this book. The four phases of teamwork we will analyze are: (1) the formulation of hypotheses, (2) the conduct of the session, (3) the therapeutic intervention, and (4) the evaluation of therapy. Each phase can be regarded both as a distinct event and as a process; consequently it can be analyzed both from a static and a dynamic point of view, if therapy is considered as a whole.

Chapter 2 | **HYPOTHESIZATION**

DEFINITION OF THE CONCEPT OF HYPOTHESIS

The concept of *hypothesizing* was officially introduced as a tool of family therapy in the article "Hypothesizing-Circularity-Neutrality" (Selvini Palazzoli et al. 1980a). That work, which together with *Paradox and Counterparadox* is one of the main theoretical contributions of the Milan group, confirmed the active interest characteristic of this therapeutic approach in the epistemological issues, borrowing the concept of hypothesis from a much wider scientific contextual framework. The epistemological issues were interpreted so as to take into account the specific requirements and goals of a therapeutic context.

Our concern here is in establishing what exactly is meant by hypothesis in family therapy, particularly within a systemic-cybernetic model. The goal is to lend "scientific credibility" to our therapy, highlighting its attention to the methodological issues and the theoretical foundations of our interventions.

The model we have adopted regards the concept of hypothesis as the *devising of models* by which reality is interpreted, contrived through an extensive and constructive use of *analogies*. Consequently, we attribute to our model an extensive and constructive significance with regard to theory, in accordance with the model-oriented theories of the philosophy of science (Hesse 1966). Such interpretive models have their own logic and make a constant reference to practice, namely to the purpose for which they were devised. This is an epistemological position close to instrumentalism and conventionalism: A hypothesis is never simply true or false, but can be judged coherent and significant with reference to a specific theoretical context, and valid or useful with reference to practice (the requirements of therapy).

The difficulties encountered in choosing a clear and univocal theoretical definition for what we mean by "hypothesis" have convinced us to opt for an instrumental definition that will be unsatisfactory for the most demanding scholars, but that fits if priority is given to therapy. In fact, the goal of therapeutic hypotheses is change, not truth. Therefore they present differences in form, substance, and even in the criteria for evaluation, from scientific hypotheses constructed for a more general purpose. In order to arrive at a definition, we have chosen to characterize the scientific process as a communication activity. Among the functions fulfilled by scientific hypotheses we favor two, upon which there could be sufficient consensus: to raise some questions (problems) and to provide some answers ("maps," theories, or connections between events).

We define a hypothesis as a statement introducing differences, namely setting facts in order, in response to a specific problem. This definition enables us to outline the way that a systemic or "circularistic" team frames and uses hypotheses during the course of its work.

CHARACTERISTICS OF THE CYBERNETIC HYPOTHESIS

A few important aspects characterizing the concept of "hypothesizing" as a tool of systemic-cybernetic epistemology can be highlighted. Our definition can be divided into three specific remarks concerning a hypothesis:

1. Since it is a statement, it is communication.
2. Since it introduces differences and sets facts in order, it is a map.
3. Since it is formulated in response to a problem, it is a proposed solution for it.

THE HYPOTHESIS AS COMMUNICATION

According to Morris, the inventor of an interesting meta-science,[1] science is above all "a set of written characters and spoken words (Morris 1955). In other words, science has the characteristics of communication, meant as transmission of information inside a system (the scientific community).

---

[1]Metascience indicates a scientific discourse on science. In the wake of the neopositivists' attempt to realize a scientific approach through the sentence-analysis method, Morris broadens Carnap's references to semantics and syntax with the addition of a third reference, pragmatics, which introduces the historical-social dimension into scientific considerations of science (Morris 1955).

In the therapeutic field, this observation is even more true since therapy implies, by definition, a dialogue and a confirmation between two interlocutors. As the therapist formulates his hypothesis on the problem at hand and on the therapeutic relationship, so does the patient formulate a hypothesis in relation to the situation. These hypotheses are included, more or less implicitly, in the communications exchanged between the two.

Following the traditional classification of Morris, later adopted by the authors of *Pragmatics of Human Communication*, the the therapeutic approach based on the theory of communication can be divided into three sections: syntax, semantics, and pragmatics (Watzlawick et al. 1967).

Syntax is the part of Morris's metascience that deals with the form or "grammar" of scientific statements. To limit ourselves to therapeutic hypotheses, we can affirm that, since they are structured as statements, they can be interpreted on the basis of a code in accordance with those rules and conventions governing common language and those characteristic of family therapy and of systemic-cybernetic theory.

Semantics concerns itself with the relation between signs and objects—with meanings. Therefore, a second set of rules, also of a conventional nature and shared by a certain social group (in this case, family therapists), sets the relation between names and events. These rules are closely tied to the therapist's theoretical background and world view, and the social and professional groups he or she belongs to.

Morris's *pragmatics* was based on the observation that hypothetical and interpretive statements are an integral part as well as the product of scientific practice. In family therapy, the hypotheses formulated by the team during the pre- and postsession discussions are tightly linked to the technical choices, interventions, and all that the therapist does and says during the session. To the field of pragmatics in therapy belong problems of the conduct of the session, the relation between psychotherapy and other human activities and between therapeutic and non-therapeutic institutions, as well as the thorny problem of the unity of procedures, goals, and effects of clinical work. Even these aspects imply specific, albeit not always explicit, rules. Stressing this last focus has been important for family therapy, since the primary goal of a clinician is to connect theory and practice as a condition for effective intervention.

One of the reasons that persuaded the Palo Alto group to favor pragmatics over the other two aspects of communication was the fact that a communicatory approach to disturbed behaviors proved remarkably useful in psychopathology. In fact, attributing the nature of "messages" to all human behaviors makes it possible to include even the "manifestations of mental illness," those behaviors traditionally considered symptoms, in a context that provides them with a meaning, and thus to regard them as adaptational behaviors within that context (see Chapter 1). This model, which in every respect may be considered a "new paradigm" (in the sense in which Kuhn [1962] used this term) represents in our field an alternative to the mechanistic-causal model of traditional psychopathology in which, when facing any behavioral manifestation, a particular form of physical determinism urged a search for its causes (genetic predisposition, early experiences, traumas, and so on).

This new model, certainly unusual both in psychology and in psychiatry, was introduced by a work we have cited more than once and that for family therapists has already become a classic: *Pragmatics of Human Communication* (Watzlawick 1967). In emphasizing the pragmatic approach, the authors brought their model of intervention closer to the behavioral one. For our purposes, the most important feature of this model is its circularity, emphasizing the interaction of all the behaviors and messages in the system under study. Bateson, unlike the Palo Alto group, does not show a great interest in the distinction between behaviors and meanings: Once more such a division reflects the dualisms permeating Western thought, the main one being that between mind and body. The Milan group, more influenced by Bateson's messages than by the pragmatic approach, resumed the analysis of the problem of meanings and expectations in therapy, closely examining the concept of world view, which embraces individual premises, the definition of oneself and others, the rules applied in interaction, and the meanings attributed to certain contexts and situations. The self-validating premises are also at the root of "pathological" behavior: Altering them means fostering change (Bateson 1972).

Regarding the hypothesis as communicative behavior within a system means overcoming the ancient, paralyzing dualism between facts and scientific hypotheses, or between the deductive and inductive conceptions of science. In a circular approach, both the inductive choice—according to which reality comes first in the scientific process, and thus the observation of facts must be privileged—and the deductive choice—which ascribes to theories, formulated by man, the power to create scientific reality—become arbitrary. When facing such alternatives, the only possible course of action consists in refusing the choice of one to the detriment of the other. This way of viewing the problem reveals all its usefulness in our field of study: In psychological experiments the interaction between the experimenter and the subject cannot be entirely eliminated, just as in clinical interviews the interaction between therapist and patient, between "hypotheses" and "reality," cannot be removed (Haley 1971, Harrè and Secord 1972, Watzlawick 1967). In particular, as a social situation the therapeutic relationship sheds a new light on all the behaviors of both interactional partners. These behaviors are reciprocally correlated. It would therefore be presumptuous on the part of the therapist to think that he/she can unilaterally influence this retroactive chain of which he/she is only a link.

THE HYPOTHESIS AS A "MAP"

The hypothesis–construction process functions, above all, as an orientation. Borrowing the map metaphor from Bateson (1972, 1979), we can ask ourselves, "Which parts and features of the territory are represented on the map?" In other words, how is a hypothesis constructed?

Our hypothetical constructions are never made up of things or events, since they cannot be experienced in themselves; *de facto* we can only experience ideas of things and events. Furthermore, if the territory were perfectly uniform, the map would solely represent its boundaries— that is, the "discontinuous event" in the perceptive-cognitive field. In fact, since every cognitive act is based on a distinction or comparison, perception can only be triggered by differences; indeed, one can say that the learning process consists of such a "perception of differences" (Bateson 1970, 1979, Ruesch and Bateson 1951).

These observations, however, do not imply that differences are "something which exists in the territory" (Keeney 1979); on the contrary, they are connected to an active, (re)structuring intervention on the part of the perceiving subject, in our case the therapeutic team. In this respect, Bateson (1979) gives the example of tactile experiences. The gradient, those small differences that make us perceive an object as smooth or rough, for example, can be created by the very movements of our hand. "The unchanging is imperceptible unless we are willing to move relative to it. . . . We *draw* distinctions; that is, we pull them out. Those distinctions that remain undrawn are *not*" (Bateson 1979, p. 97). Thus, drawing differences means giving "data" an order, a structure, so as to get the most information out of them. Only a few of the possible differences, however, are selected to become *information*, that is, "differences that make a difference" (Bateson 1970, 1971, 1979). Not every difference is relevant, at a given moment, for determining a choice between different alternatives.

"Information" in a systemic-cybernetic approach is a specific concept not to be confused with the more everyday sense of "transmission of meaning." "Meaning" is more complex, influenced by a range of factors concerning the value attributed to the information by the Mind that elaborates it. Information, instead, is a more primitive concept: It concerns the degree of freedom of the receiving system to choose, in a given situation, within a repertory of messages, signals, and symbols. More precisely, we can say that information denotes a lack or decrease of uncertainty, to which it is inversely correlated.

The hypotheses formulated by the therapeutic team during the sessions we can regard as useful punctuations, as ways—particular, idiosyncratic, focused on a purpose— of conceptualizing and describing the phenomena observed in the family. The usefulness of punctuation lies with the fact that it is structured so as to obtain or create the most information—that is, order and structure—and thus a decrease in the uncertainty and chaos to which the family therapy sessions would otherwise naturally tend (Selvini Palazzoli et al. 1980a). If the therapist were to play the role of a passive observer, presumably the system would impose its own punctuation, proposing again the usual functioning model with no information at all for either the therapist or the family. If instead the therapeutic team takes an active role in the construction of the hypotheses to be used as guides in the course of its observation and description of family patterns, the material obtained from the session will be more organized and structured. Furthermore, according to our premises, the family system receives from them an unexpected and improbable input—in other words, it changes.

This way of approaching the meaning of therapeutic hypotheses finds its theoretical foundations in a law borrowed from physics and applied by analogy to family systems, according to which a *system naturally tends towards entropy* unless it is supplied with a structure in the form of matter, energy, or information (Miller 1965a,b,c, Wiener 1965). According to the second law of thermodynamics, entropy tends to increase in time, while its opposite, negentropy or information, tends to decrease. As Miller has stated, the total information in a system can decrease without an increase elsewhere, but it cannot increase without a decrease somewhere else (Miller 1965a,b,c).

More recently, however, the application to living systems of the second law of thermodynamics has undergone severe criticism. It has been suggested that the isomorphism between the model and those systems might not always exist. Some authors—Maturana, Varela, Prigogine, von Foerster, and others—have begun to validate a totally different model. According to them the distinguishing characteristic of living systems is precisely the creation of order without any external contribution of information (Dell 1982, Elkaim 1981, von Foerster 1962, Prigogine and Stengers 1979). As therapists we cannot ignore this hypothesis; being aware, however, that its adoption in family therapy requires it to be more useful than the preceding one for mapping family systems. Experimentation concerning this hypothesis is currently in progress (in our center, too), but it is still too early to draw any conclusion. For this reason we will cling, as previously stated, to the "orthodox" model.

The identity of information and negative entropy implies that the decrease in uncertainty in the course of therapy represents an increase of information for the therapeutic team (this is what occurs in the cognitive process), and that the simultaneous introduction of additional information structures (or restructures) the system. Once more the circularity of the therapeutic activity is highlighted: Constructing hypotheses means getting to know the situation, but the system thus (re)structured, in turn sends back information, exerting its influence on the hypotheses.

In summary, the construction of hypotheses in family therapy makes it possible (1) to organize the data and the contents provided by the family, identifying differences that make a difference (namely isomorphisms between the hypotheses of the team and the hypotheses of the family); and (2) to systematize the subsequent gathering of information. This operation enables the team not only to understand the problem but, most importantly, to intervene. In fact, even the action, and thus therapeutic practice itself, can be considered as a "transformation of differences" (in a Batesonian sense); and these are exactly the differences the therapeutic team constructs through its hypotheses.

THE HYPOTHESIS AS A SOLUTION TO PROBLEMS

The relation between hypothesis and problem is not a simple one. New hypotheses are formulated after a problem has arisen; however, a problem may be envisaged and may actually arise when previously useful hypotheses have been somehow refuted. In family therapy, for instance, a problem, just like the appearance of a symptom, can be connected to the presence of "hypotheses" or premises rooted in the family that are inadequate for the assimilation of new experiences. These thus induce a crisis in the family, resulting in nonadaptive behaviors followed, perhaps, by a call for therapeutic help.

In fields like psychiatry and psychopathology a problem-oriented or task-oriented approach may be useful. Behavioral sciences are supposed to intervene in problematical situations even if, in psychiatry, the definition of a problem is neither blatant nor automatic, as testified by the numerous surveys on the social and political determinants of psychiatric diagnoses. Family therapists themselves use the concept of identified patient[2] precisely to emphasize the process of designation underlying every request for therapy (Hoffman 1971, Selvini Palazzoli et al. 1980a, Vogel and Bell 1960).

What does "creating hypotheses" mean in a task-oriented context that stresses the practical aspect at the expense of the descriptive-explanatory one? First and foremost it implies the existence of a *definition of the*

---

[2]From our point of view, the identified patient is not an individual presenting a disease but rather that member of the family unit who, at a given moment in the history of the system, finds himself or herself marked by certain characteristics. A sort of "deviation-amplifying mechanism," as Hoffman (1971) calls it, seems to occur and foster the progressive differentiation of the "chosen" member from the others, the "sane" ones. One of the characteristics of this individual, regardless of how pathological it is, is crystallized into a symptom whose unhealthy nature relies more on the patient's and his or her family's perception than on reality. This definition evolves as time goes by; thus it is not uncommon that several such identifications occur within the same system.

problematic character in a given situation; this definition must be *clearly stated*. This is by no means automatic: Describing a symptom (especially a psychological one) objectively is not an easy task. Sometimes, during the session, it is impossible to identify a properly "disturbed" behavior, despite the declared state of suffering and uneasiness. In addition, if we shift our attention to the request for therapy, we will find that the family has many expectations, even antithetical to the obvious one that it desires the recovery of the symptomatic member. In place of this logical hypothesis, it is often preferable to use the hypothesis according to which the family indeed fears the change occurring within and asks the therapist for help in stopping it. This hypothesis, which is paradoxical since it supposes that the system comes into therapy in order *to leave everything as is*, has proven more informative and has on several occasions originated effective interventions.

The difficulties in definition can be tackled by adopting an expert-style behavior, by establishing some *precise aims* through an explicit bargaining with the members of the family, and then carefully choosing the most adequate tools for the attainment of these specific aims.

In a task-oriented approach the *evaluation* of the hypotheses, and consequently of the therapeutic interventions based on them, plays an essential role. However, the meaning of this verification differs widely from that of the "positive sciences": In the cybernetic paradigm a nonverified hypothesis is as useful as one that has become true down to the smallest details. The evaluation, in fact, is based more on the achievement of the aims than on a concept of truthfulness or falsity of the interpretations made: A hypothesis in any case gives information, making it possible to construct new hypotheses and hence to proceed toward the therapeutic aims. These may be considered at a "meta level" with respect to the more specific targets of every single hypothesis.

HYPOTHESIZATION IN FAMILY THERAPY

According to Hoffman (1981), "the most important contribution of the Milan group may not be their most visible signature, the systemic paradox, but their detective work in devising a hypothesis that will explain the symptom in the family and how all the pieces fit" (p. 293).

The three concepts of *hypothesizing*, *circularity*, and *neutrality* were introduced to allow for a practicable connection between a rational and informative conduct of sessions and a powerful therapeutic intervention. Furthermore, they were intended to make the teamwork consistent with the theoretical premises. In particular, the hypothesis connects the various types of information that circulate within the team since it shares both the nature of theory (to which it is tied in the language and in the choice of the contents to be privileged) and the nature of practice (to which it is tied by its necessity for coherence with facts). For these reasons it is considered the central moment of the session, the one that more than any other justifies the intervention, with which it has a circular relation: The systemic theorizing inspires the observation and provocation of the phenomena which in turn call for a comparison with theory (Selvini Palazzoli et al. 1977b).

HYPOTHESES IN A CLINICAL CONTEXT

The hypothesis in family therapy answers, first of all, the need to rationalize clinical activity so that it is no longer left to chance or to the therapist's abilities alone. *Intuition*, *sensibility, charisma,* and other such terms with their vagueness have created an aura of black magic around psychotherapy that, as such, cannot be taught and is considered ascientific by the more "mature sciences." The need for greater scientific rigor in clinical work (and in all psychology) is not a recent one, nor is it a prerogative of our approach. The problem is hard to solve since psychology and psychiatry are still largely descriptive sciences and lack both a coherent set of clearly stated theories and some data-gathering methods adequate to the object of study. This has aroused an unprecedented interest in epistemology; even those clinicians who do not directly concern themselves with epistemological problems end up making a choice (a bad choice, as Bateson would say). The choice of a therapeutic model implies a conception of "mental disease" as well as of the tools of change, and, ultimately, of the world.

Classical psychiatry itself supplies an epistemology, the Aristotelian one. According to this, human behavior follows causal laws like every other natural event and is determined by the quantifiable properties of the individual (traits of personality, genetic predisposition, experiences, and so on). For example, in this conception of mental disturbance, schizophrenia is a characteristic of the patient that may present itself with variable (and thus potentially measurable) levels of disturbances; the goal of therapy is the reduction of this disturbance.

The "model based on complexity" is founded, instead, on the concept of *pattern which connects* (Bateson 1979, Dell 1980b) rather than on the isolation of measurable variables, and refuses the "metaphors of matter, force and energy " (Keeney 1979, 1982), which are regarded as unsuitable for this type of territory. The conception of schizophrenia that has been proposed is profoundly different, since the definition of the unit of study is different:

Over there it was the individual and here it is the familial, or social, system.

The statement that every scientific discourse, being metaphorical, is arbitrary retains its validity. As a result, the choice of this new model does not mean to be a statement of truth, but only taking a stand tied to the practical usefulness that the model has (thus far) evidenced. The biggest problem encountered by clinicians is a practical one, and in fact it is precisely in relation to the practice of therapy that the relevance of hypothesization is to be found. In its first formulation, it was not considered in a philosophical sense as a conjecture made for the purpose of understanding reality, but rather as a tool to act on reality in order to solve some problems. In this sense the concept of hypothesis may be viewed as a valid substitute for the more traditional one of *diagnosis*.

In a systemic perspective, it makes no sense to intervene on behalf of a single individual, nor to formulate a psychiatric diagnosis, intended in the sense reported by Keeney (1979) of "ascribing a label to an individual in order to signify the particular pathology and class of symptoms exhibited" (p. 117). Since the origins of the word "diagnosis" can be traced back to the word for "knowledge," one can affirm that therapists are diagnosing every time they are intent upon gathering information on a given problematic situation. However, this is not enough: This way of viewing the therapeutic relation is too unilateral and it is still influenced by the linear epistemology that regards the therapist as "he who provokes" and the patient as "he who reacts" in a passive manner to the solicitation. A step forward consists in considering the therapist as a part of the therapeutic system. Hence the diagnosis becomes a process, one that is not carried out on the individual or on the family interactions but on the interaction between the therapist and the family system. It is not possible to evaluate the family situation other than by seeing how the family responds to therapeutic interventions (Haley 1971).

Selvini and her staff, well aware of this, had proposed to substitute the verb "to be" (in reference to the family) firstly by "to seem" and lastly by "to show" (to the therapist in that situation) (Selvini Palazzoli et al. 1978). This (potentially endless) contraposition of verbs should be useful in avoiding the linguistic conditioning that leads us to believe that we "really know" the family. Thus, during the session the family appears to the therapist in a way that depends not only on its internal relationships but also on the phase of therapy.

In conclusion, there is no break in continuity between diagnostic moment and treatment in family therapy. A complicated interactional process takes place in which the therapist, by means of particular and arbitrary punctuations (hypotheses) of the situation, conforms, step by step, his or her interventions to the family's feedback. It should now be clear that such definitions as "schizophrenic family" or "psychosomatic family," which in turn are proposed as alternatives to the individual ones, simply constitute a change in the object but not in the epistemology with respect to traditional psychology; the disturbance is considered once again as an inherent quality of a real object. Hypothesizing instead is not reducible to such a labeling activity, nor is it purely descriptive or classificatory. It is a model of relations and at the same time it provides the team with an indication for the intervention, for it includes the family, the therapist, and the relation that has formed between them.

THE CONVERGENCE OF INFORMATION IN THE SYSTEMIC HYPOTHESIS

Each time the team meets, it can avail itself of a series of information coming from three different areas:

Premises of systemic epistemology.

Research experience and therapeutic practice.

Specific information relating to the case.

PREMISES

The hypothesis formulated by the team must be systemic—in other words, it must be relational and provide all the messages regarding the problem with a circular structure, so that it can be linked in a somehow significant manner to the familial rules (Selvini Palazzoli et al. 1980a). The so-called triadic hypotheses, those establishing a circular relation between the interactional behaviors of three members of the system, are typical examples of systemic hypotheses (see "The Family Game," pp. 52–55).

This does not imply that during team discussions, which end with the formulation of the hypothesis, only hypotheses that are "perfect" and consistent with systemic epistemology are voiced. Western culture, the method of dealing with daily problems, the language itself that we use, are all bearers of a linear epistemology, of a natural tendency to view things in a simple, causal, or purposive way. This attitude can be noticed also in family therapists, even though habit may bring them, in time, to think in an increasingly circular manner. Teamwork forces a comparison of different hypotheses and punctuations, even the linear ones, until their dialectical contraposition results in a global vision of the familial problem in all its complexity.

In this respect, one can assert that the pre- and postsession discussions constitute an occasion for Learning II: The polarity that develops between alternative punctuations forces the team to work at ever-higher levels of complexity; only in this way do different alternatives become compatible.

EXPERIENCE

We have previously defined hypothesizing as an application, to a certain territory, of an available model, of a metaphor that links it to a preexisting inventory. Even in family therapy one no longer works blindfolded: After decades of experience, several interpretative schemes that may be used by any team for the construction of hypotheses have now been codified. A few of these models have a high theoretical connection, as for example the double bind theory (discussed under "A Model Based on Complexity" in Chapter 1).

Once certain conditions have been singled out, disposing of a similar model allows the construction of hypotheses with a certain degree of forecasting power. If, for example, a 9-year-old child manifests the typical communicatory behaviors that organic psychiatry labels as schizophrenic, one can hypothesize that the members of the child's family will habitually send contradictory messages, whether in defining its own internal and external boundaries or in defining the reciprocal relationships. Hence every symptomatic member finds himself in the predicament of never knowing "whose side he is on" (according to the double bind theory, the symptom becomes a way of communicating without clearly defining oneself with respect to the others). The formulation of this hypothesis has repercussions on the aims of therapy: Inducing the family to define its relations in fact becomes one of the immediate goals of therapy.

In summary, according to its authors' intentions, the double bind theory should have provided a model to be applied following the observation of certain signal behaviors. These ambitions have now been for the most part abandoned by those dealing with research, although the double bind concept still proves adequate (at least on a descriptive level) in many situations.

Since the first research activities at Palo Alto, the ambitious and somewhat naive project of singling out precise family typologies to be put in connection with the presence of a certain symptom has been set aside (Watzlawick and Weakland 1977). Such an interest suffers from the effects of an excessively linear approach, even if the use of the symptom as an indicator, at least initially, may be useful in choosing the area of relations to be investigated during the session in order to "unveil the family game." An example of quasi-typological studies on a specific symptom is provided by Selvini Palazzoli's research on mental anorexia. In a monographic book on this subject, this ingenious therapist describes the anorexic symptom from different angles and shows a pattern of "family with anorexic member" that paves the way for a series of possible interventions. To cite an example, one of the rules of such systems the author has singled out is the forbidding of direct leadership, so that the power acquired by the symptomatic member is acceptable only because it is "pathological" (and by definition free of individual will). A series of possible interventions are given to modify this rule (Selvini Palazzoli 1978a).

A set of hypotheses also derived from research activity on families, and now generally accepted, concerns the temporal connections between symptoms (appearance, worsening, improvement, shift, and so on) and the *family life cycle*. There are times in the history of the system when the appearance of one symptom rather than another is more likely, and the important events (the acquisition or the loss of a member, social advancements, moves, and so on) often go hand in hand with family crises, appearance of anomalous behaviors, and the like (Haley 1973, Hoffman 1981). According to this hypothesis the symptom is a signal denoting some difficulty in overcoming a certain stage of family life.

Finally, the personal experience acquired by the therapeutic team contributes in creating a repertory of schemes, of analogies with preceding cases, of punctuations and interventions that have proved useful in the past. However, establishing these analogies is possible only in the presence of precise indicators, clues or signals suggesting the advantages of one hypothesis rather than another. We have thus reached the third point.

SPECIFIC INFORMATION

The idea underlying the systemic team's work is that one never has zero information, but in every case there is sufficient information to construct a working hypothesis (Selvini Palazzoli et al. 1980a). Even during the first encounter between therapist and family certain data concerning the case are available thanks also to the systematic use of a telephone index card for gathering the first information.

The type of approach adopted by the family in contacting the center is itself a precious source of information: The person that makes the initial call, for example, may be considered the one "that feels the worst," the system's internal contact person, or (and this hypothesis does not exclude the preceding one) the person most interested in keeping the relation with the therapist under control. Sometimes, it is not a family member but the referring person (the family doctor, an individual therapist, or perhaps a friend) who calls for an appointment. This fact by itself provides a few clues on the relationship between the referring person, the identified patient, and the family system. Furthermore, a certain insistence on the part of this person may arouse suspicion about the motivation of the family members to enter into therapy (many families that come to the center to appease someone else subsequently require enormous effort to be recruited). In any case, the problem of the relationship to be established with the referring person is one of the thorniest in family therapy. Being based on a clear definition of the context, it cannot abide the ambiguities connected with the presence of a plurality of therapies, and in any event it must deal with the "relational game" in progress between the family and the referring person (Selvini Palazzoli et al. 1980b).

THE HYPOTHESIS

During the presession the team formulates the initial working hypotheses. Generally, they pertain to (1) the therapeutic context, (2) the system to be taken into therapy (the definition of its boundaries), and (3) the family game.

THE THERAPEUTIC CONTEXT

From the point of view of the theory of communication, the request for therapy appears above all as a proposal of a relationship with the therapist and is presumably consistent with the family game.

This observation is indirectly supported by the fact that in many cases the request for therapy does not coincide with the appearance or aggravation of the symptoms but follows an improvement which, however, the family members do not seem to notice. In fact, they act as if the change under way (a "positive" one, for us) were dangerous and therefore somehow to be neutralized, perhaps by emphasizing the identification of a "patient" by a request for therapy. Consequently, instead of a tool for the attainment of change, therapy paradoxically becomes an element feeding the system's homeostasis. Before undertaking any move to implement therapy, and even before looking into family relationships and symptoms, one must analyze what going into therapy together and in such a particular context as ours (a hospital) means to the family, and how this fits the requirements of the family game.

Hence, an accurate *contextual analysis* becomes essential: It is the context that gives a meaning to the communication behaviors and consequently to therapeutic activity itself (Selvini Palazzoli 1970, 1984). This implies that the rules and *markers* inherent in that particular context, and in no other, must be introduced. This work is carried out rather slowly, but it begins with the very first telephone call to the center, when the family is first brought into contact with a world fairly new to it. The manner itself in which the operator replies to the caller's requests (legitimate and otherwise) introduces the first rules: for example, the refusal to grant an immediate interview or to meet the particular demands concerning the date and the time of the first appointment. The rule is "appointments are fixed according to the center's schedule."

One important rule concerns the referring person: If he or she is phoning on behalf of the family, he or she is kindly told that appointments can be fixed only if personally requested by one of the family members. Likewise, no particular definition of the problem must be given a great amount of attention, though such information must be taken into account during the interview.

The most important rule of family therapy, *the participation in the sessions of all the cohabitants,* is also introduced during the first contact. The caller may raise some objections to this. It is crucial that the therapist be firm and clear about this rule.

A rule that will be strictly enforced during the course of therapy is that private interviews between single family members and the therapist are not allowed (apart from a preliminary general introduction to the problem), as well as no revelations in confidence or "gossip." This would scarcely provide useful information, and the therapist would also lose his neutrality and be viewed as the confidant of one particular family member. For the same reason, the therapist abstains from giving advice or interpretation or making diagnoses outside the session (for that matter, also during the session).

This approach to dealing with the system is associated with an attitude reflecting acceptance, often a positive connotation, and at the same time clarity and lucidity. However, everything must be recorded, keeping in mind that the definition of the problem, the collected information concerning the system, and the inventory data themselves are not necessarily true and will require accurate verification at the first session.

At the Centro per lo Studio e la Terapia della Famiglia at Niguarda Hospital, where our clinical research takes place, the therapeutic team devotes special attention to context analysis. These therapists, in fact, have been trained at the private center that Selvini and others founded in Milan, and have later been called on to work within a public-service context, and hence to face new and specific problems regarding the definition of the context that required technical adjustments in the old model. In particular, a public organization must cope with engagement difficulties, negative connotations due to the fact that the interviews take place at a hospital, and complex relationships with the referring persons and other health service bodies (let alone the problems arising from the affiliation with a large institution).

The first session (a single session is often not enough) is devoted to dealing with all of these aspects, the so-called context cleaning, and to the clarification of what the service can provide, so that some real contextual hypoth-

eses can be formulated—and subsequently the appropriate interventions carried out. This enables a clear
definition of the therapeutic relationship by means of the
introduction of context markers, by calling on other
members to take part in the sessions, and in a few cases
by refusing to take the system into therapy. These
definition-sessions are no different from the others, save
for their content: Both the conduct of the interview and
the construction of the hypotheses follow the usual criteria. Indeed, it may happen that a whole therapy is a
"therapy of definition" of the therapeutic context and
that, as soon as the family has clearly defined its relationship with the therapist, both the request for therapy and
the problem from which it has arisen come to an end.

A classic example of the threats that may come to the
context is provided by the failure of one of the members to
attend a session in spite of an explicit convocation of all
the cohabitants. This is a potentially disqualifying message, an attempt to introduce a rule that may eventually
lead to the "death" of the therapeutic relationship, that of
unpunished disobedience.

In such a situation the team may decide to hold the
session all the same, defining it, however, as an "informal
interview," thus avoiding a symmetric reaction and at the
same time reaffirming the rule that only therapists can
make certain decisions.

Over and beyond these observations, a member's absence must be taken into account, on the basis of the
general principle according to which every event within
the family depends on the reciprocal fitness of the parties
involved, and thus cannot be put into a merely causative
relation with the will or the power of a single family
member ("He refused to come").

When hypothesizing on this event therapists must ask
themselves who is going to get the most advantage from

this absence? Is the system scared by therapy? And, above all, how can the system be reassured, so as to induce the absent member to attend the sessions?

As far as the referring person is concerned, it is important that some hypotheses be made with regard to the circumstances under which the family has been sent to the center: Did he leave them, or is it a so-called dirty trick, a referral with no adequate preliminary role-clarification? And, above all, did the recommendation for family therapy result in a weighty designation of the identified patient's parents or partner?

THE SYSTEM TO BE TAKEN INTO THERAPY

One of the aims of the first session, generally defined a consultation session, is to decide who makes up the system to be taken into therapy. If the system is regarded as being made up exclusively of those individuals living with the identified patient, thus limited to the persons attending the first session, several hypotheses on the game can be constructed, taking into account all the possible triads within the family unit. If a wider definition of system is adopted, and the relations with the environment are taken into account, the number of the possible triads increases dramatically. In this case, the therapists can, or rather must, take into consideration anyone who may be viewed as a mediator in the family relationships and thus somehow involved in the reckoning within the family. The most likely candidates are relatives, friends, referring persons, teachers and all the different kinds of therapists. Each of them sends messages to the family with regard to the problem (and most importantly, with regard to the therapy they are about to start), and acts as crisis "stabilizer" or "amplifier." In both cases, he or she becomes an essential element for a thorough comprehension as well as solution of the problem (in this respect, it is advisable that therapists bear in mind that they may find themselves playing such a dual role and that they should therefore take into account the pragmatic effects of every move they make in the course of therapy). At the end of the first session, it should be possible to draw a very accurate map of the "family territory": family tree, friends, working conditions, and so on. At every stage of therapy, however, the system's boundaries as set in the first few sessions must be monitored and, if necessary, readjusted.

THE FAMILY GAME

We shall now focus our attention on the "real" therapeutic hypotheses, those concerning family relationships or the "game" which, as we have seen, is the target of therapeutic intervention. The principle of circularity (Hoffman 1981) has led therapists and theoreticians to adopt a triadic marking both in formulating their hypotheses and in determining the style of the interview (see Chapter 3). It has not always been so: The first research activities on communication emphasized the exchange of messages on a diadic level, as witnessed by Bateson's "schismogenesis" (Bateson 1935, Bateson et al. 1956, Sluzki and Beavin 1965, Sluzki et al. 1967). It soon became clear, however, that such an analysis was not thorough and complex enough, since it did not take into account the presence of a third party in many cases of greater importance than those immediately identifiable in relation to a given interactive sequence. The study of triads (Haley 1969, 1971, Hoffman 1981, Selvini Palazzoli 1978, Weakland 1960), which implies a higher level of complexity but is nonetheless attainable for our limited analytical abilities, was thus undertaken (Selvini Palazzoli et al. 1983).

Representative examples of "triadic" hypotheses are those concerning coalitions, particularly denied coalitions. In human systems, coalitions involving two people hostile to a third can be easily identified, unless they are denied on another level of communication. This is the perverse triangle hypothesis formulated by Haley (1969): Since denied coalitions prevent metacommunication from taking place, they are "pathogenic" for the members involved, who are thus forced to resort to ambiguous messages and to undefined (in other words, symptomatic) communication. Therefore, the symptom can be regarded as the outcome of a coalition that spares any disagreeable feedback since it is not directly and explicitly controlled ("It is the symptom, not I, that has the power"). A multiplicity of coalitions, even of a conflicting nature, can be identified within a given system: This is the advantage of denial.

Another example of a triadic hypothesis is the one viewing the symptom as the calling back of a fugitive member. From the symptomatic member's point of view, his or her behaviors may be a test of the relationship with an important figure, while from the point of view of the other members it may appear to be induced by someone for the purpose of controlling the relationship with somebody else. In this respect, one may say that the relationship relevant to the construction of the hypothesis is not the one the symptom seems to indicate, and that the identified patient simply plays the role of mediator in the family game.

A typical case is that in which the symptom bearer is a child or teenager, whereby one can devise a perverse triangle between the father, the mother, and the son or daughter and hypothesize that the latter's problem allows the parents to avoid beginning a discussion or more precise definition of their relationship.

However, we must emphasize that these hypotheses, complex though they may be, do not fully account for the complexity of reality, and that their relevance therefore lies with the fact that they allow the therapist to identify a target for intervention.

The strategy to be adopted in the interview, the topics to be discussed, and to a certain extent the format of the questions to be asked during the sessions, are chosen in line with the hypotheses. The hypotheses' circularity ensures the questions' circularity, while good hypotheses (good at least in the therapists' opinion) ensure the impact of the questions on the family game. It is essential that the hypotheses not be entirely gratuitous: They must somehow be isomorphic or comparable to those of the family, since only thus is refutation possible. Constructing refutable hypotheses (to which the system may respond in such a way as to force the therapist to discard them) means implementing a "scientific therapy." The first requirement of the team, therefore, is flexibility, for at any moment they may be called on to start all over again in the event some undisclosed facts or elements contradicting the initial hypothesis are brought to light. This is particularly true with reference to the first session, as one must not forget that preliminary information is provided unilaterally. A problem may be thoroughly redefined in the course of therapy, according to the then prevailing hypothesis.

Such a flexibility in the definition of the problems during the therapeutic process implies the team's ability to reconsider and, if necessary, reformulate its hypotheses (this is one of the supervisor's tasks). Besides, this reflects the nature itself of systemic hypotheses: Maintaining a hypothesis unchanged for several sessions (thus being consistent in conducting the interviews and in the intervention) is extremely dangerous since it may imply that the therapist has gotten involved in the game, has entered a coevolution with the system, as Bateson would say (Bateson 1979, Dell 1982), thereby losing any therapeutic impact. Paradoxically enough, the hypothesis that has worked, that has given birth to a change in the system, becomes unusable and must be reviewed if not abandoned. Here the cognitive process really appears as a constant refutation of every hypothesis constructed; what is never refuted becomes the contextual framework where hypotheses are placed.

CLINICAL CASE: A SYSTEMIC TEAM DRAWS A MAP

In the following pages, the start of a complete therapy is presented through the verbatim transcripts of selected parts of the first session. These have been transcribed word by word from the recordings of the therapy. Comments are also included to explain, step by step, the therapeutic team's actions, so that the reader may experience in vivo how therapists from the Milan school work with families.

The subsequent sessions of the same case will be given in Chapters 3, 4, and 5, in each instance at the end of the chapter. This subdivision is justified by the fact that in each of those chapters the reader will find the theoretical conceptualization of what takes place in that particular session.

THE OSBURM FAMILY

In May 1983, Mr. Osburm repeatedly calls the center requesting urgent therapy for his son Benjamin, who for several weeks has been refusing to attend school. The problem soon appears to be much graver than a simple "scholastic phobia," since the child displays behaviors that, according to traditional nosological categories, are defined as psychotic: aggressiveness, introversion, refusal to leave the house, and neglect of one's favorite activities and personal hygiene. Furthermore, the family's history is a difficult one: The parents had separated for a few years and subsequently reconciled, but with a rather unique arrangement.

As we will see, from the very first session the therapeutic team discards the possibility of working on the bearer of the symptom, and instead takes the remaining family system into therapy. This decision together with the intervention techniques is responsible for the symptom's complete remission after just three sessions.

THE INFORMATION CARD

During a presession interview with Mr. Osburm the following data were gathered and recorded onto an information card:

Date of the first call: (May xx, 1983)

Family: (name, address, telephone number)

Who made the initial call? Father

Why did they call the Center: The youngest child for the past 15 days has been refusing to attend school because it makes him sick

Information on the sender: (Name, address, how did he or she contact us)

Map and notes on the family structure and the cohabitants' subsystem

Father: William, 33 years old, office worker, high school diploma

Mother: Joan, 32 years old, office worker, high school diploma

1st son: David, 11 years old, 5th grade

2nd son: Benjamin, 9 years old, 3rd grade

(We have no information on the rest of the family)

SUMMARY OF THE PRESESSION INTERVIEW

Benjamin no longer wants to go to school because it makes him ill (strange feeling in the pit of his stomach, knot in his throat). The appearance of the symptom coincides with his mother's departure for a short trip. Initially, Benjamin was supposed to accompany her (so the parents had agreed); when he changed his mind, David went instead. Several attempts have been made to reassure him at school but all have failed.

The parents had been separated, by mutual consent, for two to three years, and the father had been awarded custody of the children; the mother could see them at will. Her visits had been frequent until one and a half years earlier the maternal grandfather had died and Mrs. Osburm, together with the maternal grandmother, moved into Mr. Osburm's house. Since then, Mr. and Mrs. Osburm have lived together again.

William feels that, on certain occasions, Mrs. Osburm is not accepted by himself or his sons. He also says that he and his wife often criticize their respective extramarital relationships (Mr. Osburm before the separation and Mrs. Osburm afterwards); they had separated because she had a lover.

FIRST SESSION: ABSENCE OF THE IDENTIFIED PATIENT

THE PRESESSION DISCUSSION

During the presession conversation, the therapists draw a map on the basis of the available data.

S (supervisor): It seems that the mother and father got back together when her father died.

T (therapist-conductor): Yes, and they also took the mother-in-law with them. . . . Doctor so-and-so sent us this case, he says it's extremely urgent; they wanted an appointment before the end of school.

S: They may be worried that Benjamin will flunk out. . . .

T: You mean they *were* scared: School is over now.

S: They may not even come, if they got that situation straightened out. . . . The rest is too messed up for them to want to deal with it. . . .

Their hypothesis is that other problems are concealed behind the symptom, and that the system is not willing to deal with them. The rush might only be the son's possible flunking out; in this case, the family might really not show up since, in the meantime, school has ended (the therapists notice, at this time, that the family is late for their appointment).

T: The deal here is really complicated because the grandmother didn't just move in for a few months, *she moved in for good*.

This hypothesis is expressed in linear terms, but it is nonetheless useful because it makes a connection between the behaviors of the mother, father, and maternal grandmother. In systemic terms, there is a connection between the parental couple's reunion and the grandmother's moving in. This raises a few questions on the grandmother's role in the family system and of her role with respect to the symptom.

At this point of the presession interview, the family arrives at the center: just the parents and David; Benjamin, they say, did not want to come. Nowadays, he never leaves the house.

T: He doesn't even leave the house?

S: This is absurd! Parents who cannot even convince a 9-year-old child. . . .

T: (member of therapeutic team): They should tie him up and bring him anyway!

S: Of course, no two ways about it! Are you kidding?

The supervisor does not intend to accept the system's disobedience—the appointment had been scheduled for all the family members. This behavior is a bit too rigid though consistent with the model: A corresponding reaction, in other words, and a refusal to conduct the therapy would not have been a smart countermove. Later on we will see how this obstacle could have been avoided and the session conducted without letting the family take charge so boldly.

S: Any other family members to speak of?

T: We do not know. Let us begin. I shall send someone to fetch them.

S: Yes. What are we going to do?

T: Let us try to understand. . . . In your opinion, this symptom . . . ok, so the pretext is that *the mother is going away on a short trip*. What can have happened?

S: I don't know, it looks like a symptom in *response to the mother's return*. . . .

Two important connections are established: The first is ascribed to an event that might have occurred at the same time as the appearance of the symptom (the mother's departure); the second, instead, is connected to an event from the past but nonetheless an important one for the family (the parents' reconciliation). However, maybe too much time has elapsed for such a direct link.

T: A symptom in response to the mother's return, but why so late? The mother has been back for over a year.

T: She might be *threatening to leave again*.

T: It isn't very clear here, really. "She leaves for a trip," what does it mean? If she is moving. . . .

The therapist is wondering about the real meaning behind the mother's departure. Is it really a "short trip" or just another "trial separation?" On a verbal level, it appears to be a veritable, "justified" trip (for health reasons), but on an analogical level one should know what message has reached the husband and children.

S: Yes, but it seems that the child refused to go with the mother.

T: He did refuse, his older brother went instead.

S: Then, *she can leave only if escorted by a "body guard,"* this is a nice bit of information. Hence, the child might become symptomatic in order not to escort her. In other words he might be refusing to take part in his father's game.

This is a hypothesis based on a triad between father, mother, and Benjamin. Initially, a "bottom-line" observation is made: In spite of Benjamin's refusal to accompany her, the mother had an escort.

Hypothesis: Someone somehow wants to keep an eye on her at all times. This someone might be the father: There have been problems between the two, and maybe there still are. This hypothesis is quite a common one when the patient is very young, but in this case it is also justified by the presession interview with Mr. Osburm. If this hypothesis were accepted, Benjamin's symptom might be the outward expression of a denied coalition with his mother against his father. Since it is not handled in the first person ("the symptom has power over me, not vice versa"), it protects one from dangerous retroactions.

T: They keep on leaving him at home, who stays with him?

S: No one, I guess, or maybe his grandmother.

T: We have to get this grandmother business straightened out.

The information available on this is a bit hazy: Does the grandmother still live with them? Do they see each other often? Do they live by each other? Might other relatives be involved with the problem? On the basis of these questions, the therapist decides to take advantage of the family's presence to answer a few questions. Thus, they will hold the session anyway but explain that its only aim is to gather information.

S: We might even discover that the grandmother lives with them now and that we should have scheduled her for the session, too. . . . We have no definite knowledge to assure us that the family is composed of only four persons. The grandmother might spend long periods of time with them; in this case she is as much a family member as all the others. We don't know this for sure. We shall ask for information like this, saying that a veritable session is not possible due to Benjamin's absence. . . .

T: When someone stays home, *that is who is most afraid of coming,* but also *who controls the situation:* a 9-year-old boy who refuses to accompany his mother, refuses to go to school, and now refuses to come here. Then we have this grandmother who seems to have reconciled the parents. . . . It says so right here that she went to live with them for a few months. . . . In other words she put them back together and then left. Hence *it's possible that there are problems on this level* (mother, father, grandmother triad). If there are any problems on this level, it is highly probable that the identified patient *is developing a psychotic reaction.* Thus, it might also be a *symptom of a very serious psychotic transaction.* If the family is also psychotic it will not only have *enormous difficulties in defining relationships but, most of all, boundaries;* in other words, it is an undifferentiated family. Since this is the first session, one must draw a family map, or at least a map of how the family was in the past few years. Consequently, we must make a historical and temporal reconstruction of the boundaries, cohabitants, grandparents, grandchildren, sons, etc.

At the end of the discussion, the team has identified two triads: father-mother-grandmother and father-mother-son. The hypotheses on both these triads point to a pessimistic prognosis on the family communication and hence on the symptom.

What is the information to look for during the session to verify these hypotheses? All information pointing to serious problems within the couple—that is, confused communication behavior between the parents and between the parents and children, and reluctance in accepting differences within the system. Another type of information that will be actively sought during the interview concerns the enlarged family: If it plays an active part in the system's life, to the point of determining its course, this would justify the initial "gut feeling" that we are dealing with a "psychotic" system.

THE SYSTEMIC TEAM TESTS ITS HYPOTHESES ON THE FAMILY

Going along with the definition of the session as an "informal conversation aimed at the gathering of information," the therapeutic team decides not to study the problem or the symptom any further. In this stage, the therapists, as we have seen, consider the following items of primary importance: (1) the family map and (2) information about the people who gravitate around it ("those who are aware of the problem," "those who give advice," and "those who try to solve it, and in what way").

An additional piece of information soon emerges, which reveals that the maternal grandmother (though not living with them) and Mr. Osburm's family were perfectly aware of the situation. In fact, they had all tried to advise and intervene with the child in order to solve the problem. Another important piece of information is that Benjamin stays home alone: He is not only self-sufficient but able to prepare a meal for his whole family, to make small repairs around the house, and so forth. (These are the first signs of a behavior not fitting a 9-year-old.)

F (father): My mother thinks . . . her advice is to . . . in a way she minimizes the problem.

T: In other words, there isn't a problem.

F: No, there is a problem!

T: But his grandmother says there isn't.

F: Yes, but she also says that "Like many other things . . . maybe it is the product of a traditional environment. . . . I don't really know."

T: Yes, and she is also of a certain age . . . wise, not wanting to waste any time. . . .

F: (He interrupts.) Exactly! I mean: "You'll see, it will go away. Just give it time. This is summer, and then it will be . . . time enough for him to recover."

T: (Interrupts.) So this is what your mother says, while instead? . . .

F: She is worried, but at the same time full of hope, optimistic regarding something which I, instead . . . I can't see how it can be so, they're just her hypotheses . . .

T: (Interrupts again.) You mean with respect to your hypotheses, which are a bit more pessimistic than your mother's?

F: Yes, yes.

T: And then? Who else? What about the other grandparents?

F: I don't know. . . .

M (mother): (Interrupts.) Well, my mother has tried punishing him. He really wanted a ten-speed bike, he really did, and his grandmother (she looks towards her husband) who had promised she would get it for him . . .

F: (Surprised and appalled.) So, that's why! She did not buy it because . . .

M: Yes, she also told him "If you go back to school, I shall buy you that bicycle, right away." This was at the beginning, but it didn't work, because the child didn't care about the bicycle. He said "I feel sick when I go to school . . . so I don't care about the bicycle." And from that moment, he has not gone to visit his grandmother. Or rather, he does not come with us, isn't that right David? (Looks at her son.) From that time on.

F: Never?

M: Never. He refuses to come.

D (David): That's right.

F: Are you sure?

M: He's never gone to his grandma's after that. As a matter of fact, David and I went to my mother's to eat . . .

T: And he stayed at home.

D: Yes.

Later on, when talking of the little authority they have over Benjamin, the mother will say: "In fact, yesterday he told me, 'Look, Joan, don't beg me.' I said, 'But I am not pleading, I am just inviting you to come to grandma's. I don't want you to stay here alone. Also because . . . .' 'But when I'm home alone I watch TV, listen to music, I am not bored.' "

An important item of information concerns the mother and indirectly the couple:

T: Do you go visit your mother often, or does she come to your house?

M: No, we usually go on Tuesdays and Thursdays because she rests on those days . . .

T: Two half days. In the afternoon?

M: Yes, in the afternoon and we usually eat there.

T: Supper?

M: No, lunch . . .

T: (Interrupts.) How can you go for lunch on weekdays?

M: Well, my husband doesn't come, just the children and myself.

T: (Interrupts.) Well . . . but you work also . . .

M: *I always work the night shift.*

T: You always work the night shift?

M; Yes.

T: Then you always work at night?

M: I always work at night.

T: Is it possible? I mean to work the night shift all the time.

M: I chose to work at night, myself.

T: (Interrupts.) Yes, but, even if you decided yourself, is it possible?

M: Yes, it's possible, yes, very easily.

F: (Puzzled.) *I think it's strange, too.*

M: (Interrupts.) I had chosen this shift because I had problems . . .

F: I mean, the unions should not allow a person . . .

T: (Interrupts.) Yes, I thought so, too. . . . But, of course, if she is doing it I guess you can.

M: Well, if I do, excuse me William, it's because it's possible.

F: Well, there are many things we shouldn't do . . .

T: (Interrupts.) Thus, you work the night shift, *you work five nights a week?*

M: *Six nights a week—I also work Saturdays.*

Later on, Mrs. Osburm will say that she had chosen this shift in order to spend more time with her children. But something is "fishy": Ever since the couple reconciled they have never led the "life of a couple" because of her work schedule. On the other hand, on an analogical plane the husband's puzzlement over this situation is quite clear.

Another crucial moment in the session is when information concerning *denied coalitions* surrounding the symptom arise:

T: (Talking to David) Do you like to go to school?

D: Yes. Yes, I like school.

T: What about Benjamin?

D: Not as much. (He laughs.)

T: Why?

M: (Intervenes.) But he's always had this problem, hasn't he? (Looking at her husband.) Isn't it so, William? He never liked going to school. . . . (The husband does not seem to agree.) Let's say that *sometimes* (she looks at Mr. Osburm, who nods and tells her to go on) *he did not want to go to school, he would say, "Hide me, please,"* because he knew his dad was stricter than I was, and . . .

T: Hide him from whom? From his father?

M: (Laughing.) From his father, yes. In the morning . . . I used to take the kids to school . . . he would say, "You take David, and then hide me at your aunts' house"; I have these aunts who live in the country, about five miles from us. He would stay practically the whole morning with the dog . . .

T: (Interrupts.) Thus, at times, you would hide him at your aunts'?

M: Well, yes I did, *I hid him at my aunts' house.* (David laughs.)

T: (Interrupts.) You would tell your husband . . .

M: (Interrupts.) No, *I would tell him in the evening,* "Benjamin didn't go to school today, but *please don't tell him I told you because I promised I wouldn't say anything.*" This must have happened ten times or so during the school year. The next day he would just go to school regularly.

At this time, Mr. Osburm gives a pretty serious summary of the behaviors of the patient and of the failed attempts to make him return to school. His pessimism is, in addition, worsened by the fact that he finds his son's behavior changed also with regard to the way he spends his free time: He never leaves the house, he even refused to go to the soccer stadium (he is a fervent soccer fan), and he refused to go to the shore on vacation . . . and now he won't come to therapy.

T: What do you think Benjamin expects you to tell him when you go home?

F: When you called me about this morning's appointment, I asked Joan "How should we tell him?" because I had a feeling it was going to be a problem. I had already talked to Benjamin about Doctor so-and-so [the referring person with whom the parents had met a few times before coming to the Center], and he had refused to go: "I'll pick my own doctor." But then he had seemed to change his mind. . . . By then, however, I had contacted you, so I told him, I was very careful, "Doctor so-and-so has sent us." On the contrary, that's not how it went, if I remember correctly he thought we were going to Doctor so-and-so, in Milan. When I told him "Milan," he said "Milan, no, I am not coming to Milan." "Why not? Milan is not . . . your mother and I always go."

The supervisor calls the therapist on the phone to suggest he backtrack a little and get more information on "where" and "to whom" the child was told he would be going.

> T: You mean, Benjamin thinks you came to Doctor so-and-so?
> F: Yes.
> T: Hence, he doesn't know you came to a center, etc.?
> D: No, he doesn't.
> M: (Interrupts.) But we later explained to him that it was a center.
> F: No, we later explained . . .
> M: (Interrupts.) That you were doctor so-and-so.
> T: (Interrupting, slightly appalled.) I am Doctor so-and-so?

At this point, Mr. Osburm states that he had thought it was irrelevant to explain to Benjamin which doctor they were going to. The parents' previous appointments with Doctor so-and-so had also been kept secret from the identified patient. The deceptions, however, are not over yet.

> T: Now, when you get home what will you tell him? That you spoke to . . . that I am Doctor so-and-so?
> F: (Interrupts.) I put the problem like this: "Look, Benjamin I took half a day off work, I've already paid a certain sum . . ."
> T: (Interrupts.) Who did you give money to?[3]
> F: No, no, I mean this is what I told the child.
> M: You told him that? (She laughs.)
> T: You told him that . . .
> F: I don't know what to do anymore; I mean we don't know what to tell the child.
> T: In order to make him come here?
> F: Exactly.
> T: Wouldn't it have been easier just to pick him up and carry him?
> F: I can't do that.

---

[3]The Centro per lo Studio e la Terapia della Famiglia at Niguarda Hospital is free, but Mr. Osburm told this lie in order "to convince Benjamin to come."

T: Not even the three of you?

F: I mean . . .

T: (Interrupts.) You say that you have made all these attempts to convince him, to get the four of you here. Did your wife agree that Benjamin should also come, or did she say "Oh, just let him be?"

F: Oh no, she agreed he should come today, too.

When questioned about Benjamin's expectations of the session, the parents are not in agreement: Mr. Osburm thinks that he will be expecting something (he doesn't say what), Mrs. Osburm, instead, thinks he will not be expecting anything nor will he ask any questions (the manner she uses to convey this denotes that she thinks she knows and understands her son better than her husband). However, when the therapist asks them how they will behave, the father says he will be "adamant." "You didn't want to come, I don't see why you should be interested." The mother, instead, replies, "But in this way, you will be rejecting him, and he will feel even worse than he already does." (Later on, she adds: "He will ask questions.") An additional remark: David did not speak much during the session; each time he prepared to speak, his mother would interrupt and answer for him.

POSTSESSION HYPOTHESES

The hypothesis that one (or both) parents *were scared of bringing the patient* was confirmed by what did emerge. We have noted, in fact, the existence of "denied coalitions," in other words, a much stronger tie with the patient than has been admitted (this hypothesis is also confirmed, through analogy, by the control they seem to exercise on David). An additional confirmation also comes to us from the lies and booby traps, whose only aim (or so they said) was to get Benjamin to come, and which, on the contrary, succeeded in doing just the opposite. Ultimately, these family

"moves" provide a series of escape routes and disqualifications for the therapist, who suddenly finds himself
being someone else (Doctor so-and-so), and leave him
with new problems of definition (with respect to the
patient, the family members, and so on).

Even the hypothesis *that the couple is not really close* has
found numerous confirmations: The mother's night work
perpetuates this situation, and both the husband and wife
could also derive advantages from having a symptomatic
son (the father in order to remind his wife of her "guilt":
abandonding her children, cheating; the mother to avoid,
even if she has "returned to her family," defining herself
with respect to her husband and her children).

The generational boundaries appear thin and not well
defined: The children call their parents by their first name,
the patient, in particular, seems to take on a parental role
(that is, he does little jobs around the house, cooks meals
for everyone), and the remaining family members also
take an active part in the system's life. All these observations seem to confirm the gravity of the symptom. Such a
situation is common in systems with *ambiguous and confused transactions*. If we were to refer to typologies, we
would have to say this is a psychotic transacting family. If
we had investigated the game surrounding the symptom
(which we chose not to), the function of the symptom with
respect to the father would also have emerged.

HYPOTHESES ON THE INTERVENTION

In order to formulate a veritable therapeutic intervention,
information on the game (which we do not have) and,
most of all, the patient's presence are necessary. Each
decision that does not take this into consideration is
bound for defeat, because experience teaches us that *the
absent member has the power to annul all therapeutic inputs*.
After all, a veritable intervention would not be coherent
with the definition of the interview as a "nonsession."

A possible conclusion to this session might be to send everyone back home, call another session for all the family members, and cross one's fingers in the hope that next time they will obey. In this case, however, all the family members will be very scared and the therapists will be convinced that they are, most certainly, going to drop out. Hence, a message to reassure them is given, they are told not to worry because the therapist's chief concern is not Benjamin (this is called "problem shifting"—see Chapter 4) and at the same time they express their concern for the gravity of the situation ("dramatization").

THE INTERVENTION

We will limit ourselves to transcribing the intervention, without commenting upon it, since for the time being we are solely interested in the verification-refutation process of the hypotheses.

T: As we had mentioned earlier, as a result of someone's absence, today's session has been used for gathering information. Benjamin's absence per se is of no consequence, since this would have been the outcome if any one of you had not come. In the meantime, however, we would like to tell you that on the basis of the information you have given us, on what has emerged during today's talk, but most especially on the basis of experience, not only of this center but of others like it, hence on statistics of cases like yours, which are not as rare as you all might think; if we should ever worry, and we are, we think that we should be more worried about David, since in situations like this there is the risk that, somehow, what we call, quotes, the "symptom," might be transferred to David.

We are telling you this, and we have discussed it a long time and have also looked back at similar cases to be sure, because though we are not able to give you any information on your situation in particular until we have seen all the family members, we would like to warn you that, on the basis of similar cases and statistics, we are worried about David and we thought you should know.

We must now verify this idea, and we hope we shall be able to see you next time, to begin, as we always do, with a consultation, and eventually, with therapy if that is indicated.

THE CONDUCT OF THE SESSION

Chapter 3

In this chapter we will attempt to give a few general indications concerning the planning and conduct of a family therapy session. Consequently, this chapter will be, in a sense, more technical than the preceding ones. However, everything that takes place during a session must have theoretical and methodological justification.

It would be both simplistic and misleading to consider the correct formulation of questions and final interventions as the main objective of training in family therapy. Instead, acquiring the capacity to formulate systemic hypotheses and to work while bearing them in mind is much harder but infinitely more useful. In order to intervene effectively, however, it is necessary to familiarize oneself with the techniques that facilitate therapeutic work. For this reason, a family therapy session run in conformity to the systemic model is conducted in accordance with specific criteria, which in turn are linked to the functions of the session and to the characteristics that make it "a session of systemic family therapy."

We are talking about the criteria of *plausibility* and of *novelty*, which are two complementary properties of communication.

PLAUSIBILITY

In order for a family, or any other system that processes information, to assimilate the therapist's punctuations, there must be a redundancy between these punctuations and the family's own interpretations of the situation, of the problem, and of how it should be resolved. The criterion of the plausibility of hypotheses may be translated into a need to draw, during the session, an accurate map of the family, of the contents that it considers relevant and of its own construction and interpretation of reality. Hence, an initial "hook-up" takes place that lays the foundation for all that is to follow and makes it comprehensible. The therapist's punctuations (even the more arbitrary ones) are accepted because they are introduced as if the family itself had suggested them (at least with regard to content, since our modalities are generally more circular and neutral than theirs would have been).

NOVELTY

The hypothesis that the therapeutic team translates into questions for the family must promote change. This means that new information is fed to the system (which "naturally" tends toward entropy) from the outside in the form of differences, which interact with the system's current structure, allowing it to find a new equilibrium that no longer requires the symptom. The mechanism that permits this change to take place is the positive retroaction.

This model of change that has sustained our clinical and research activity is, as we have already said, in a critical reelaboration phase by epistemologists, scientists in various disciplines (von Foerster 1962, Prigogine and Stengers 1979), and clinicians like Dell (1980b, 1982). Having adopted the concept of "order through fluctuation," Dell rejects the idea that a family system is characterized by equilibrium, and relies instead on the concept of evolution intended as a continuous passage between various stages of nonequilibrium. These passages occur through the fluctuations, even little ones, of a given system. They are unexpected, highly influenced by chance, and by definition irreversible. According to this concept, the therapist's activity is seen from an entirely different point of view: A model is not imposed, since the system is what it is and could not be otherwise (a "real" input, a novelty, would have such a violent impact as to destroy the system). But that is not all: The very concept of novelty becomes unreachable, since it is more a category of the observer than a property inherent to information. How should our therapeutic input then be fit into Dell's model? The system behaves according to its organizational coherence and evolves according to its structure. Each move made by the therapist is a medium or something expected by the system's fluctuation. (Medium is to the system what background is to the figure: It contains and sustains it.) The aim of therapy is no longer change but acceptance of the system's reality—being in harmony with the system.

THE CONDUCT OF THE FIRST SESSION:
AN ATTEMPT AT GENERALIZATION

We have decided to stress the first session since it presents a few distinctive problems that, once resolved, will not reappear for the remainder of the therapy. In addition, being the engagement session, it is devoted for the most part to the installment of a therapeutic relationship and the creation of premises on which the effectiveness of all our future work is based.

The rules governing therapy—context markings, neutrality, triadic questions, and a professional attitude in dealing with the problem—are all new experiences for the system, which then modifies its expectations and premises in favor of others more functional to the successful outcome of the treatment.

Each subsequent session must then insert itself into the framework based on trust, acceptance of the rules, and willingness to change, which the therapeutic team has been laying the groundwork for from the very first interview with the family. Hence the first session is a decisive one both because of the need to define the therapeutic relationship and to guarantee the system's openness to the interventions.

The first session is called a *consultation session* in order to give the therapist ample time to respond to the request for therapy. Numerous possibilities exist, including that of refusing to take on a family whose engagement might prove too dangerous.

From a methodological and formal point of view, however, the first session is identical to the subsequent ones. Or better stated, each session maintains in part the goals of the first: The context's definition is never taken for granted, and the dangers of disqualification are always present (in particular, after an especially destabilizing intervention for the system). The definition of the problem itself may be revised at any time.

What happens when the therapist enters the therapy room? The first step consists of introducing oneself and getting the family acquainted with the setting. The new surroundings (which include a one-way mirror, video recorders, and microphones) and the length of time required (the session itself lasts one hour, in addition to the team discussion and the final intervention) require an explanation. We then proceed with the inevitable question: "What's the problem?" This question is open to all and to none, even from an analogical point of view. It is used to give the system ample time to answer and also to introduce, right from the start, the therapist's neutrality. Furthermore, his or her attitude, which is one of acceptance of what the various members may think, is emphasized by the fact that the therapist does not stop with the first response but goes on to ask the other members what they think.

In addition to this initial question, there are other typical areas that require investigation during the first session. Although these cannot be reduced to a simple questionnaire, it is nonetheless possible to list the topics that will most probably be touched on.

THE PROBLEM

By definition, the first session entails framing and describing the problem. In addition, bargaining may also be necessary, since the system's various members may have differing opinions, or we might find ourselves confronted by multiple designations. (This is very rare, however, with patients with a psychiatric diagnosis, since they are the problem, or rather the symptom, which almost acquires a personality of its own.) Sometimes during the first session the history of the problem is investigated (not always, since it weighs down the designation) and particular attention is given to the analysis of solutions attempted and the interpretation of failures.

MAP OF THE SYSTEM

Before engaging the family, it is important to decide which system to summon. Hence, a careful study of the relationships with the enlarged family and maybe even the referring parties, teachers, neighbors, and friends will also be required. It is important to understand both the quality and the quantity of the relationships, how close to the family they live, and all other clues of possible involvement.

THE EXPECTATIONS

Expectations are mostly used to evaluate the motivation level and to identify the members most "dangerous" for therapy, those willing to disqualify the therapist in order to "save the game." During the intervention, differing expectations should also be taken into consideration, to prevent the engagement from automatically becoming a coalition between the therapeutic team and the system's "internal contact person." A question that needs to be answered is: "What did you expect by coming here today?"

THE THERAPIES

Finished therapies and, more important, those still under way, should also be investigated. One should be careful not to disqualify the mother's, father's, or somebody else's personal therapist. Colleagues should always be favorably evaluated in order to avoid becoming the third element in the system's game with the other therapist.

FAMILY RULES

In order to work on the problem, one must first determine its connection to the rules of the game, who is most benefited by the symptom, and which communicatory patterns sustain it (keeping in mind that the rules we identified are descriptive metaphors). The first session usually does not get into these areas, which are the ones on which the whole course of therapy will be based. In fact, before any therapeutic action can take place, all of the requirements touched on in the preceding paragraphs must be satisfied.

THE SYMPTOM

Almost inevitably the first session becomes a time for the family to discuss the symptom. When our patients come to the center, they have expectations regarding the definition of the problem as psychological, individual, or whatever. Since their problem is identified with the patient they prepare themselves ahead of time to describe, in the smallest details, all of his or her pathologic behaviors (in addition to thoughts, motivations, and intentions), and to convey their anxiety and powerlessness in dealing with them.

Quite often, people come to the center with a complicated past history of referrals, diagnoses, and medicines that, from their point of view, is useful knowledge for the therapist and the subject of never-ending discussion. If they succeed, the therapist is inundated by data, recriminations, self-accusations, and sometimes cries in a generally anxious and desperate atmosphere.

The therapist, however, has little interest in learning of the symptom's individual aspects, and thus actively intervenes by asking circular questions that tie together the system members' relationships, to extract the most information out of the system. Research on the symptom will thus be limited to the relationships and differences between the patient, his or her relatives, and their attitudes toward the patient.

In a systemic hypothesis, the symptom is correlated with the system's performed behaviors; to modify it would mean acting on the family's perception of the symptom (which sustains it) and on the stereotypes that deny differences.

Thus, questions having the symptom as its object have two goals: (1) changing certain already structured definitions and (2) revealing those who need the symptom. Probably everyone needs the symptom to one degree or another, but someone, according to the hypotheses, is the key element. If we consider the symptom as a message addressed to at least two members of the system (triadic hypothesis), it should also be clear that one of the intermediate goals of therapy is to identify and understand its behavioral effects. By discovering how the various members react and interpret the symptom, we can also find out who is most benefited by it. This person, nonetheless, should never be blamed or invested with causal responsibility; usually both the symptom and the behavior that supports it are positively connotated.

How can a study of the symptom proceed concretely? When studying the symptom, one of the most important questions is asking the people to describe it in *specific behavioral terms*. The aim of this request is to obtain a change of definition of the symptomatic member—from "he or she is crazy," "he or she is mean," "there is something wrong with him or her," to "when this happens he or she reacts like this."[1]

What start as personal adjectives become actions, and hence increasingly subject to control and, furthermore, circumscribable to precise conditions. Similar request are in fact always accompanied by a *specification of the circumstances*: time, place, frequency of behaviors, and above all, who is present at the time and how he or she reacts.

One must not forget that a triadic hypothesis underlies such questions. For example, if the identified patient were a young boy, the triad F-M-S would almost certainly be probed for the purpose of establishing whether the symptomatic behavior is an expression and/or a cover-up for a denied conflict between the parents. A model question might be: "When your son behaves in this way, what does your wife (or husband) do? Do you agree with her or his reaction?" It is most important that *differing behaviors* between different people emerge—for example, between the parents or between the parents and grandparents. These differences might emerge sooner if the various participants were asked to compile lists on the basis of

---

[1]This interviewing technique is found in Selvini Palazzoli, Boscolo, Cecchin, and Prata's "Hypothesizing-Circularity-Neutrality" (1980a), but its roots stretch even further to observations made by the first researchers of human communication. In fact, it has been observed that it is quite common (not just in "pathological" families) to transform what a person does into a sort of personal quality or trait: this is quite economical, but it often becomes a self-fulfilling prophecy to the point that even if the person behaves differently each action he or she performs is permeated by the attributed quality. In the case of a "mental disorder" label, this process is particularly evident. The person designated as "mentally ill" is considered such in every context and moment. In reality, the so-called unadaptive behaviors are always limited by time and space, and manifest themselves in precise situations. They must be explained; and the adjectives must return as actions and processes; only thus can the problem's definition change (Bandler and Grinder 1975, Dell 1980). The basis for this and similar techniques is the idea that language determines reality. According to this concept, being able to make people express themselves differently means making them think differently.

higher or lower degree of worry, aggressive reaction to the symptom, or the capacity or inability to feel empathy towards the identified patient. The question the therapist really has in mind is "Who is most involved in this vicious circle in which the symptom represents the stabilizing factor?" These lists may be requested also on the basis of attempted solutions or of different circumstances at different times: "Did the problem seem more or less grave after Mom took that decision?" "Who felt better before?" "Who's feeling better now?" (Penn 1982, Selvini Palazzoli et al. 1980a).

A symptom may also be analyzed through its *temporal connections* (not causal) with meaningful events. Quite often, marriages, flights, births, and deaths are connected with the appearance of the symptom in the patient also because these events are conducive to guilt feelings. Less common, instead, is the link between the patient's behaviors and its effects on the system: modification of certain habits, behavior changes in a family member, return of a "fugitive" member, and so on.

One last observation: A symptomatic member and all that he or she entails on a social and personal level often makes one lose the sense of time. In the anxiety attendant on a situation that is viewed as having no way out, the system also loses its sense of the past and especially of the future. *Hypothetical questions* are thus used to project a bright ray of sunshine in an otherwise bleak future. The family system must be made to hypothesize different solutions and various responses to the symptom, perhaps tied to decisions that involve an ever-wider system.

Nevertheless, neutrality should prevail during these "symptom investigation techniques." The symptom is a minefield for therapeutic neutrality: By talking about it one runs the risk of weighing down the designation (and losing the patient), and also of increasing the parents' sense of uneasiness and inadequacy, not to mention the fine disqualification towards all those that have somehow had to deal with the problem without being able to resolve it. For these reasons, although the disappearance of the symptom is a good indication of a successful therapy, we are little interested in knowing all of its aspects; on the contrary, we try to shift the focus to something or someone else.

FUNCTIONS AND CHARACTERISTICS OF A FAMILY THERAPY SESSION

It will be useful here to consider what the various functions of a session are and how they are met.

First of all the therapist tries to *obtain information* on how the various family members perceive the situation (never information on how it "really is"). They are punctuations, mainly expressed in a linear form, and the therapeutic team's task is to compare and contrast them and then make the necessary connections.

Furthermore, interacting with the family enables the therapist to introduce the rules of the setting, to respond to the attempts of breaking these rules, and in general to define himself as an "expert" on the situation.

Lastly, the session serves to *anchor the relational patterns.* This is called *tracking,*[2] which consists in reintroducing the same information provided by the family that, in the meantime, has been linked together (according to the

___

[2]The term *tracking* can be translated both as "following a track" and as "mapping out a route." In fact the therapist's questions correspond to both these functions. The importance of tracking consists in its ability to transfer to therapy Bateson's idea that reality cannot be changed unless it has been constructed, and that reality is constructed through social interactions (in our case, therapeutic relationships) (Selvini Palazzoli et al. 1980a).

hypothesis) so as to introduce differences or information. In a sense, it is a true reconstruction of reality as the family perceives it, and may be an alternative to the dysfunctional premises that have guided it until now. This function is fulfilled by the informative questions, which we have already discussed and will take up again shortly.

Tracking is the equivalent, during the session, of the negentropic or information-providing function of the systemic hypothesis (see Chapter 2). It is a powerful change agent, and if it serves in creating presuppositions for the system to "accept" the final intervention, one can legitimately wonder whether it really can be considered a therapeutic tool as such. (This hypothesis, which is found at the end of "Hypothesizing-Circularity-Neutrality" [Selvini Palazzoli et al. 1980a], could be easily verified by eliminating the closing intervention and identifying therapy solely with the conduct techniques.) With respect to other techniques centered on paradoxical intervention, tracking may be considered a distinguishing technique of the Milan model of family therapy; it is what most differentiates our work, which is based on premises, from that of strategic therapists, which focuses on the problem instead.

CIRCULARITY AND NEUTRALITY OF THERAPEUTIC WORK

Hypothesizing, circularity, and neutrality were born at the same time as criteria for the conduct of the session (Selvini Palazzoli et al. 1980a). It can be said, however, that although hypothesizing has acquired a position of prominence, circularity and neutrality have been characterized more as concrete translations in technical terms of the therapeutic hypotheses, rather than as concepts having a life of their own.

What is meant by circularity? It is a fundamental property of systems, the basic principle of both von Bertalanffy's holistic paradigm and Bateson's cybernetic one (see Chapter 1). More specifically, circularity is a requirement of the therapist, a fundamental aspiration of the therapeutic process, and the ground of its effectiveness. Selvini Palazzoli and associates define it, in relation to therapeutic practice, as the "therapist's capacity to conduct his investigation based on the family's retroaction to the information he has obtained through the relationship, in terms of differences and change" (Selvini Palazzoli et al. 1980a). From a theoretical point of view, the principle of circularity in the conduct of the interview is consistent with Bateson's view, according to which we only think in terms of relationships and differences (Bateson 1972, 1979).

The concept, embodied in a series of interviewing methods that are really a tool for the creation and collection of differences, has several interesting technical angles. Above all, circularity means being able to view both the therapist–family interaction and the therapist–supervisor one as processes in which each elaborated information is dependent on the relationship between the two participants, rather than on just one. In this way the therapist must simultaneously keep in mind his role within the two systems.

Another requirement of the model with respect to the therapist's work is neutrality. Neutrality should not simply be intended as an open, nonjudgmental attitude (especially on a moral plane). This attitude is quite common among many types of therapies, but what differentiates a systemic therapist from others is that he counts neutrality as a therapeutic tool rather than a norm of professional ethics. Indeed, for systemic therapists neutrality is a principle consistent with the need to define the relationship with the family in a certain way. Although the therapist is often trained as a "savior" or a "witch doctor," just as often he or she is considered a "judge," with all that the corresponding connotations imply for the family's expectations and cooperation during therapy.

If the therapist avoids accepting the obvious and stable definitions of the problem put forth by the system's members, referring parties, and others (which have themselves become a part of the problem) (Watzlawick et al. 1974); if he or she avoids accepting a more or less thin proposal for coalition with one of its members; if he or she avoids blaming the patient's parents as the cause of the problem (a common and simple enough trap), he does so not only for ethical reasons but mainly to establish consistency with the systemic model. During the whole therapeutic process, the therapeutic Mind (the team of therapists) introduces and tries to maintain a circular view of the inter- and intrasystemic relationships within the patient's epistemology. The team has to maintain neutrality; otherwise it will not reach its goal. In fact, any stand becomes a directive for the therapeutic relationship, and is more or less interpreted by the family according to the usual categories ("the therapist is on my side" or "the therapist is against me") and it reinforces their hypotheses.

In reality, however, asking a question of a particular family member implies a choice and is not neutral (also because isolated behavior may hardly be defined in a particular way, especially at the beginning of therapy when certain rules have not yet been introduced). According to our approach, in fact, neutrality does not characterize a therapist's every behavior; rather, it is a pragmatic effect of the whole session.

How can this effect be achieved?

Through a series of consecutive, "nonneutral" behaviors, such that the final sum is neutral.

Time plays an important part in our model. By introducing the time factor into a message one can totally change its meaning. The juxtaposition of event x and of subsequent event y (for example, two different persons being asked the same question) may be altogether neutral in spite of the questions' nonneutrality; the static and isolated vision of the scientific method alone can deny this observation. Hence for these reasons the more dangerous questions are in turn posed to the whole system. This tactic introduces the message that the therapist does not favor any punctuation at the expense of another, and that all differences are acceptable.

For the same reason the therapist tries to conduct well-balanced sessions: Everyone must speak for a set amount of time—not too short and not too long.

Furthermore, each member is always given the opportunity to answer back, expressing a view about what has been said about him or her.

As time goes by, the therapist establishes positive accepting relationships with each member, until the therapist's professional attitude toward the system in toto has been made clear.

Neutrality is harder to maintain when one of the members makes negative statements about the others. The therapist must not accept such statements in order to avoid a coalition with this particular member; on the other hand a net refusal implies a negative connotation for that same member. Hence one must behave in such a way that the family understands that the therapist's refusal is not aimed at the single individual. In this respect, a useful tactic might be a positive redefinition of those "individual characteristics" that the system had identified as faults, pathologies, and spite. When this is not possible, such attributions are accepted but are classified as legitimate ideas and thus, by definition, not necessarily true. A useful underlining of this attitude is obtained by immediately turning the question around to the person in question: "How do you feel about what x just said?"

Neutrality also means giving each comment, interpretation, or hypothesis made by the therapist the status of an idea. Thus, a "metaposition" about the problem is favored: In therapy the rule is that various hypotheses on the problem are simply compared, apart from their being true or not.

Furthermore, neutrality is more than just a therapeutic trick. It is a demonstration of the team's level of "systemic wiseness," the awareness of being part of a Mind or whole in which all of the members are interdependently related (Bateson 1972, 1979). In view of the complexity of systems, they cannot be reduced to a scheme and, in our opinion, it is well to avoid simple and static punctuations of what takes place within the system and thus to really consider each hypothesis as absolutely arbitrary.

Another aspect of neutrality is that attitude that allows the therapist not to blame the family when it does not respond to his "inputs" in the desired way. (Neutrality is expressed towards both the single member and the system as a whole.) There are situations in which this becomes the therapy's central issue: when, for example, the family makes moves that disqualify the therapeutic context; when it comes to the session without a member who had been previously requested to come; when the symptom suddenly worsens rather than improves; when the family members during the session openly mystify or disqualify what the therapist is doing or saying; and so on.

Being quick to review one's strategies, and never blaming the family for either successes or failures but rather placing the blame on the therapeutic team's activity, apply more to the therapeutic process than to the single session.

Neutrality is thus increasingly comprehensive. The model itself anticipates that the system's organization will determine the outcome and not the therapeutic intervention. To expect the system to react as we would like it to do is a grave epistemological error. (If it does not, it means that we were mistaken and not that the system is opposing itself.) On this subject, Hoffman feels that the concept of neutrality, as applied by the Milan school, is an expression of the new model that no longer views the therapist as a force acting on the family or patient (Dell 1982, Hoffman 1981).

However, a negative reaction to an unexpected effect would not, from a systemic point of view, be a wise move, though a human one; for this reason it is very important to work together as a team. Hence, neutrality does not become a trait of the single therapist but the outcome of the circular elaboration of data by the therapeutic Mind.

In conclusion, circularity and neutrality are but two sides of the systemic hypothesis, representing what transpires in the therapist's interaction with the family.

TEAMWORK AND CONDUCT OF THE THERAPY: THE FUNCTIONS OF THE SUPERVISOR

Our therapeutic setting envisages the simultaneous presence during the session of a "conductor" (in the therapy room) and of a supervisor (behind the mirror). This is the minimum unit necessary in order to conduct therapy following the model we propose. In fact, behind the mirror in addition to the supervisor could be a few trainees, researchers, other operators from the center, and nonprofessional operators assigned to the video recorder. Although these persons may or may not act specifically as supervisors, they often take part in the discussion. Whoever is in the supervision room has the advantage of following the session from a completely different angle, called the "metaposition," than that of the conductor. Indeed, not having to worry about asking questions or directly answering the family system's moves, the supervisor may observe the course of the session in a detached manner and from a higher (and thus more complex) logical level.

Although the therapist's tasks include not getting involved in the game, always controlling the course of the session, and remaining active, he will never completely succeed since by definition, he is an element of the system and is thus dependent, for all he says and does, on what the family has previously said and done and on its countermoves.

Thanks to the supervisor's metaposition, the supervisor is given the opportunity to notice, ahead of time and more clearly, the family's messages in relation to the therapist's messages. Hence he or she often picks up aspects of the family–therapist relationship that the therapist does not even notice, such as some very fine symmetrical moves involving the therapist in an "escalation," or slips from a one-up to a one-down position (Bateson 1935, Haley 1963, Selvini Palazzoli 1978b, Sluzki and Beavin 1965). Often a family system's frequent moves are nothing but attempts to involve the therapist in nontherapeutic roles (which are dangerous since they open the way for disqualifications of the context), and make the therapist lose his or her neutrality by proposing various coalitions.

An additional function of the supervisor is to get the therapist out of impasse situations in which the family turns out to lead the interview and gives only a minimum amount of information. Detachment enables the supervisor to formulate "metahypotheses" on the condition of the therapist–family relationship.

The supervisor's presence may also prove extremely useful with regard to context: The supervisor may in fact suggest questions on topics just discussed that the therapist has overlooked (the family often does its best to divert the interest from subjects too closely linked with the family's rules, myths, and secrets). The suggestions that the supervisor makes through the intercom system aid the therapist in making prompt and careful examinations of all the interesting information that emerges during the interview.

Furthermore, in the midsession discussion the therapist and observer meet to compare their respective points of view and to modify the hypotheses or to formulate new ones.

An additional aspect of therapeutic teamwork is the adjustment of one's target or the reformulation of a question in a more informative (circular) manner. More than a correction of the contexts, it is really a formal correction without which the therapist–conductor would easily lose his or her neutrality (conditioned as we are by linear language), or would touch upon (perhaps prematurely, and thus with homeostatic side effects) family myths, secrets, denied relationships, and so on. In summary, the three functions performed by the supervisor are (1) looking out for the conductor, so as not to make this person lose his or her "metaposition" with respect to the family system; (2) giving a specific or new input to the hypotheses; and (3) redirecting the interview to more useful questions.

A special remark must be made for budding therapists. Contrary to what usually happens in other forms of therapy, a supervisor of family therapy is on the same level as the conductor, and all members of the therapeutic team periodically exchange roles. A therapist may conduct the therapy one time and stay behind the mirror the next. This situation enables us to reaffirm the therapeutic team members' absolute equality in the formulation of hypotheses; an ideal situation, in the sense that it guarantees circularity, which is harder to acquire when the team is not homogeneous.

In a training context, the supervisor is also a teacher and thus acquires supplementary functions in addition to the three just given. A family therapy session is an extremely complex event, much more so than any individual session (at least because of the number of persons attending). In fact, as a result of unfamiliarity with the guiding hypotheses, an inexperienced therapist might very well be overcome by the contexts and relationships that emerge. The therapist might be embarrassed by the wide choice of topics for conversation, in the formulation of triadic questions, or in linking his actions to the presession hypotheses. This uneasiness diminishes when the supervisor calls the therapist to provide the missing connections and to suggest a specific behavior; more useful still is the time when the therapist leaves the therapy room for a short discussion that makes it possible to frame the situation and "recharges" the therapist for the next part of the session. He or she then returns to the therapy with a set of questions previously agreed upon with the supervisor-trainer, and the intervention becomes more effective and rational.

THERAPIST–FAMILY INTERACTION: VERBAL AND ANALOGICAL ASPECTS

Journals dealing with the science of communication usually classify human communication into two modes with differing functions, often operating simultaneously, though not always, in the same direction. These modes are (1) analogical and (2) verbal or numerical communication (Bateson 1972, Ruesch and Bateson 1951, Watzlawick et al. 1967). Each interaction is in fact conducted on the basis of two types of information: the data dealing with words and numbers, and the data dealing with behaviors and gestures that accompany the words and numbers. In addition, two neurologically differentiated codes also exist that in the course of evolution divided (though not totally) their respective areas of interest. These are the content area, for the verbal modules, and the areas of relationships for the nonverbal ones.

The analogical module is unsuitable for the transmission of precise contents, while the verbal (or rather numerical) module is totally inadequate (and by universal consent, also unreliable) for communications in interpersonal relationships.

Since the very beginning of communicatory research (which led to the "double bind" concept), the psychopathological hypothesis adopted was that schizophrenic behavior might be linked to incongruences between the two levels of communication (Bateson 1969, Bateson et al. 1956, Sluzki and Ransom 1976). An interesting factor in these hypotheses is that these incongruences were noticed in the symptomatic behavior, in the communication patterns of the (presumably sane) people interacting with the patient and finally in the therapeutic interventions that appeared effective in solving the problem. This aroused a particular interest in the family's communication style and also in the manner in which it would analogically comment on the therapist's remarks, thereby introducing in the therapeutic process a series of extremely important items of information that would otherwise be lost.

Ultimately, this means that in addition to working on a verbal level the therapist, aided by colleagues' detached observations, also works on an analogical level; in other words, the therapist gathers and makes observations not only through the contents of the questions and answers but also through the behavioral signs that accompany them.

CONTENTS

Concerning contents, one must decode the responses to the questions. It is important that contents that emerge along the way are tied to the family's "premises" in order to understand them (semantic aspect of communication).

Through the verbal behavior, the family reveals its manner of punctuating facts and gives definitions, attributions, and also clues on its world view (which is often strictly connected to the problem).

Obtaining such contents is important because it gives the family the impression that someone is listening and understanding. Quite often the family therapy session is the first and perhaps only time in the system's life that it is allowed to express thoughts and feelings about the problem. Obtaining these contents is also important because they represent the rough material on which the circular questions are formulated, and because the final evaluation of therapy cannot prescind from a thorough knowledge of the initial premises, myths, and so on.

RELATIONS

The planning of a session is, on an analogical level, a much harder task since it is closely linked to styles, situations, and chance. Nevertheless, there are areas in which the impact of this type of message is more evident: (1) information tied to an analogical plane, concerned with family rules; (2) analogical messages aimed at the therapist that propose a definition of the relationship; and (3) the therapist's use of the analogical module to introduce information and rules. We will discuss each of the three areas in turn.

Concerning the first area, since these signals are "metacommunicatory" with respect to those more interested in contents, they provide information concerning possible discrepancies, denied coalitions, and double messages that take place during the interview (and, hypothetically, also outside).

If, for example, a dubious expression or a denial sign is noticed in a member while another is giving his or her punctuation, one can hypothesize the existence of differences between the two even if they are denied on a verbal plane. Another possible case is that in which there is a deep inconsistency between a person's words and actions, as between a tragic content and a light, carefree tone. This "comment" might be a self-disqualification or an attempt at saying something while denying it at the same time. Although in more traditional diagnoses such a behavior is usually labeled as "dissociation," and is considered a symptom of grave pathologies, in our case we try instead to connect it with what has been said before, with the system's global situation at the time, and above all with those topics that the therapist's question touches upon (to discover, almost invariably, that they are taboo subjects presumably tied to the "rules of the system").

With reference to the theories of communication and the research conducted by the Palo Alto group, we may consider the discrepancies between verbal and analogical modules as disqualification and self-disqualification messages (Sluzki et al. 1967), signals of a denied coalition, denials of a denial, and so on.

An area of relations that is often and amply defined on an analogical level is the therapeutic relationship (Viaro and Leonardi 1983). In fact, both the family and the therapist use their behaviors to install, confirm, or abolish rules, and thus to accept or disqualify the relationship the other proposes. The "context markers" themselves are nothing but analogical messages on the relationship.

An attempt by the family at controlling the relationship may manifest itself through the adoption of a facetious and gossipy tone totally inappropriate to the situation, or a member's acting out during the session if the therapist touches dangerous relationships. When tears, laughter, and humorous comments appear in the session, they are a sort of message for the therapist, and in the meantime they define the relationship (both in the direction desired by the therapist and also in the opposite direction).

The therapist's analogical messages have two main functions: to give adequate context markers and to guarantee the engagement. The therapist never defines himself as one-down, unless he has a specific purpose in mind and in an intervention or in a context that is able to control the relation. In addition, the therapist never engages in symmetrical fights with the family: The therapist's goal is to define himself "meta" in relation to the family.

Neutrality itself is guaranteed by the therapist's capacity to adequately communicate his messages, even those potentially biased, as intended to aid the system in its totality and not to accuse any of its members.

The therapist's knowledge of how to handle his communications, not only the verbal ones but especially the analogical ones, becomes a powerful intervention tool. A knowledgeable use of the discrepancies between the two modules can in this case be considered therapeutic since it reveals the family game. For example, a dramatic question may be asked in a carefree tone, or a dangerous one may be introduced by a slightly quizzical tone to emphasize its hypothetical character, or something might on the surface seem to point at a particular family member while instead it is meant for another (in this case, the nonverbal module may be of much help in making the message reach its real target).

CONDUCT CHOICES

During the presession interview, the therapeutic team, having analyzed the available information (the telephone information card if this is the first session, or the session's transcripts if it is a subsequent one) and formulated the first hypotheses, comes to an agreement on how the therapist will conduct the interview.

This choice, naturally, will conform to the functions (gathering information, introducing rules, and tracing the relational patterns) and the characteristics (circularity and neutrality) of the session.

In order to conduct the interview in as rational and informative a way as possible, it is important to explicitly choose the topics for discussion and how they should be dealt with; the therapist will thus be able to maintain clear ideas and a sharp tongue. An additional advantage is the following: The more coherent and orderly the conduct is, the more it will be a learning experience for the family, whose communication style, on the contrary, is confused and incoherent.

The conduct choices refer to the areas of relationship, contents, themes, specific questions, and often inputs that the system will be given in the form of interpretations, rereadings, and comments, or simply on an analogical plane.

RELATIONSHIPS

A first choice must be made with regard to the areas of family relationships one wishes to investigate. The hypotheses themselves suggest certain areas as more relevant to the problem. The hypotheses point to the relevant and irrelevant information, thus giving a clear idea of what one should look for. We have seen, for example, that a frequent triadic hypothesis, in cases with symptomatic children, is that there are problems in defining the parental couple with respect to the children. Such a hypothesis carries with it specific conduct choices: In order to confirm it the therapist must investigate the triads, the manifested and hidden alliances between parent and child, the rules, denials, and the myths connected to them.

THE CONTENTS

With regard to the topics of discussion, which are necessary since they are the substance through which relationships manifest themselves, the therapist chooses even trivial contents, but nonetheless interesting from the family's point of view (or, each time, from the point of view of a different family member). There are, in fact, subjects they take to heart and others they expect to discuss, that help define the situation as one of understanding, acceptance, and aid. Other topics still might be dear to a system's member and help in getting him or her more actively involved in the session, "speaking the same language" and maintaining the therapist's neutrality so as not to make that person feel left out.

All the contents are identified on the basis of interest signals the family makes in reaction to the questions. Most of the time they emerge by themselves, and if the therapist feels that these signals are sufficiently informative and will not negatively influence the context's definition, he will decide to study them thoroughly. (Sometimes the therapist will deliberately divert discussions from dangerous topics, such as a detailed description of the system, medical jargon, or guilty recriminations.) In the same question, content and relation are two complementary aspects (Watzlawick and Weakland 1977): The way to gather information on a privileged relationship is to make the family members talk of something that is more or less directly linked to this relationship.

The questions that will usually solicit such information are, for example, those tied to the family's usual day (generally this question is asked of children). Though apparently trivial, such questions may bring to light interesting facts.

In order to ask such a question, one can refer back to anything that has incidentally emerged during therapy. (We do not say "unexpectedly" because the appearance of new information is always somehow tied to the conduct choices.)

The following is a classic example of how certain contents should be treated: At a certain point during therapy, the mother states, "Lately I have been very depressed." This simple phrase cannot be overlooked, but at the same time it can (and is) a "move" with simultaneous and numerous functions: a call for help; a shift of the focus onto the mother; self-guilt with respect to the father, the therapist, or someone else; or disqualification of the previous definition of the problem. The therapist's countermove must be systemic; hence it must respond to the mother's message by circularizing it or by putting it in relation both to the family game and to a given moment of therapy. During the third session, for example, when Mrs. Osburm made such a statement, the therapist asked her whether these behaviors (depression and crying) were related to the identified patient's behaviors. This counter-move also awakened the father's interest, who affirmed that "My wife's not just crying because of Benjamin; now that she has changed her job she is far too busy and tired to take care of the house." When faced with such mes-sages, verifying whether the mother is really depressed is no longer relevant, it is more important to verify how all the family members react to her depression. One's ap-proach in resolving a given problem is not important: With respect to the "model that connects," the therapeutic input is not able to modify the system's pattern but rather to catalyze its evolution, which is intrinsic in the structure and coherence that characterize it.

QUESTIONS

Selvini and her group have introduced a veritable tech-nique for gathering circular information that has proven very useful in guiding the therapist during the interview (Penn 1982, Selvini Palazzoli et al. 1977b, 1980a, Viaro and Leonardi 1983).

According to the cybernetic notion that "information = difference" (see Chapter 1), it logically follows that useful information, in this epistemological context, is that solic-ited in terms of difference (spatial, temporal, contextual, or whatever).

Informative questions are such because they have been structured circularly; in other words there is a *biunivocal relation between hypotheses and questions* (both are triadic). Questions are formulated in a particular manner in order to introduce, even if indirectly, the triadic hypotheses drawn during the presession, and as the interview proceeds also in the supervision room. The questions are asked in such a manner as to make the family aware of the differences that exist within and that it often denies. (The acceptance of differences is nonetheless secondary to certain fundamental characteristics of the punctuations introduced, mainly neutrality and plausibility.)

To convey these new interpretative schemes verbally and in a linear manner ("You are like this . . .") would serve very little purpose: The system would not understand, and at most such a message would increase the distrust and anxiety generally associated with being in therapy.

Instead, the "progressive circularizing" of the family's world-view is obtained implicitly through a series of harmless questions that nevertheless stimulate interest, and above all, metacommunicatory behaviors.

We shall now offer a descriptive scheme on the techniques of circular investigation, one that is not much different from that originally introduced by the Milan group (Selvini Palazolli et al. 1980a). (In the discussion of the conduct of the first session earlier in the chapter we have already anticipated a few of these techniques.)

Triadic questions: A member of the system is asked *how he perceives the relationship between the other two.* This question, which in turn is asked to the various members, enables to bring to light the privileged relationships and the coalitions that almost always accompany a situation of psychological suffering (see "Triadic Hypotheses" in Chapter 2). If evaluation differences emerge, they will constitute an important experience for the family and useful information for the team. (A characteristic of pathological systems is, in fact, denial of differences.) The family might even decide, at some point, to reveal unexpected problems which could become the focus of treatment.

Answers are solicited in terms of specific interactional behaviors under specific (and well-detailed) circumstances. One should never leave room for interpretations or attributions of purpose. Particular attention must be given to this rule when defining the problem and when identifying the goals of therapy. If left on its own, the system will often proffer a nebulous solution in which unfalsifiable, hence dangerous, hypotheses are wasted on personal feelings, sensations, and individuals' dispositions. Each communication behavior is colored by all the interpretations given by the system's members. Comparing these vague questions full of "psychologisms" with the communications that are exchanged before and after the session indeed becomes an impossible mission for the therapeutic team. On account of the nonobjective data, triggering change and eventually evaluating when and if it has occurred is particularly difficult.

If material of this kind should emerge uncalled for during the interview, it should be judged not as an individual's intrapsychic experience but as a message contributing to the definition (or nondefinition) of the relationship between the various participants in the interaction.

An observation should also be made concerning the "familial style": with the mass culture's interest in psychological themes (in particular psychodynamics), it is quite common to find families using terms like *unconscious motive, frustrations,* and *traumas.* In such systems, an important message may be provided by a member volunteering as an expert on this subject, attempting to form a coalition or at least to place himself or herself symmetrically with the therapist.

an evolutionary hypothesis that the system itself has formulated.)

At times, instead, images of an even more anxious and dramatic hypothetical future may induce a crisis situation and thus create, where one does not exist, a motivation to change. A crisis, in fact, is a shift in the system's equilibrium and as such it triggers a search for new behaviors. This might be positive for the system, especially if it no longer needs the symptom to function. (This explanation, however, includes problems connected to the intervention, which we will discuss in Chapter 4.)

INPUTS

The inputs that are given to the family during the session are classifiable as interventions. They are, in fact, positive connotations, revisions, restructurings, or shifts that could very well make up the final interventions. The only real difference is that they are generally introduced as hypotheses and that the system is asked to respond to the question (which never happens in an intervention) "How do you feel about our idea?"

For tactical reasons, the therapeutic team introduces them toward the end of the interview. The most immediate usefulness of inputs consists in helping to define the therapeutic relationship or in sweeping away ambiguities while at the same time introducing the paradoxical intervention (a more detailed explanation will be given in Chapter 4).

Although clinical psychologists do not usually consider their activity experimental, the session's proceedings appear to be nothing more than a test of the therapeutic hypotheses. The hypotheses are circular and formulated in order to guarantee the therapist's activity during the information-gathering process. These statements might appear hopelessly contradictory: Since all hypotheses are plausible, shouldn't perfect circularity coincide with an operative standstill?

For this reason, a choice must be made among the plausible hypotheses that will bring forth the one most useful for the intervention.[3] The ultimate verification of the usefulness of a hypothesis may only be the system's retroaction to therapy; but a correct conduct should make it possible to reduce the hypotheses to just a few coherent interventions. An additional elimination usually takes place in the postsession discussion, where the therapeutic team finally agrees on one or two hypotheses and translates them into the final intervention. (The team may also, on the basis of the information available, decide not to have a veritable final intervention; but this in itself is a strategy.) A last consideration is *de rigueur*: An important change must already have taken place in the system before the therapist-conductor leaves the therapy room.

The family should have been able to perceive, maybe for the first time in its history, its differences; it should have assimilated a few rules of the therapeutic context; it should have understood a few of the therapist's expectations; and above all it should have formed ideas regarding its problem. This process is inevitable since the family is a Mind and, as such, processes the information given from the very beginning.

CLINICAL CASE: THE FAMILY RETURNS

This section continues the case study begun near the end of Chapter 2. There the first session was conducted and reviewed.

---

[3]One never talks of true hypotheses but rather of useful ones, and useful hypotheses are those that are also informative, namely those that admit only two types of answers: a verification (the family retroacts as expected) and a refutation (the family retroacts in a manner that refutes the hypotheses). Only with hypotheses this well constructed may the last, and more difficult, stage of clinical work take place: the evaluation (see Chapter 5).

SECOND SESSION: THE IDENTIFIED PATIENT

PRESESSION

Three months have elapsed since the first session. This time even Benjamin, the identified patient, has come. During the presession discussion the therapists look over the previous hypotheses and the intervention. It looks like our method succeeded at least in bringing all the family members together; hence our hypothesis, which three months ago was "someone did not want to bring him," today becomes "someone has wanted to bring him." This session's aim is to verify the hypotheses on the area of relationships and the family game, which we were unable to introduce as informative questions the last time; in particular, we wish to discover if the symptom really is *functional to the couple* and whether it is used to avoid a direct confrontation with the problems.

Context-wise, the conduct will be coherent with the intervention, which made the *object of the session* the verification of the possibility that the symptom would shift over to David. The therapist proposes to make the children speak, Benjamin in particular, in order to balance the situation with respect to the last session and also to reestablish neutrality. Little by little, as important information arises, he will introduce circular questions.

CONDUCT OF THE SESSION

T (therapist-conductor): (Talking to Benjamin.) Let's see, after they came here last time, when they got home, what did you ask them? "How did it go?"

B (Benjamin): Well, yes.

The therapist immediately starts by asking Benjamin questions about what and how the others told him about the session and especially the intervention.

T: So, tell us, did they tell you what we talked about? What did they tell you . . . what did you think?

B: (He looks at his father and whispers to himself.)

F (father): Well, he askèd about what you thought. (Benjamin laughs.) Do you remember?

B: Oh, no! (He laughs.)

On an analogical level, Benjamin seems to be very controlled: His parents are constantly looking at him and he also seems to be looking for their approval *with his eyes.* One spontaneously wonders: "Does he have permission to talk? Did they bring him here to disqualify, once again, the therapeutic context?"

T: (Interrupts.) Well, you don't have to remember everything. If you remember, your parents and your brother came and you, instead, stayed home; when they came back, they must have told you something: "We went to . . . ." You must have asked: "So, what happened?" and so forth. I would like you to tell me about this story, about what you remember, ok?

B: Mmm. (He keeps on whispering the question over and over but doesn't answer.)

M (mother): Don't you remember anything at all? But that's impossible! (with disbelief.)

B: (He laughs.)

M: You don't remember anything?

B: (He laughs.)

M: Benjamin, that's impossible!

B: I just know that you came.

M: You just know we came? And then?

A little at a time the therapist pulls information out of him: At the end he admits that he was told something, but he doesn't say what. He does remember saying that he would not have come to this session either.

T: Then you do remember that in June when they told you, you said "No, no, I won't go." Is that right? . . . And instead, what happened today?

In view of the situation, the therapist tries to define, somehow, the patient in relation to the therapy, until Benjamin begins to communicate very strongly on an analogical level, saying with his behaviors: "I don't have anything to do with it, I'm not here." Not only is any kind of communication made impossible but each subsequent intervention may be disqualified. (The parents seem frightened at the thought that he might "compromise" himself and so they constantly interrupt.)

B: (Looks around and whispers.)

F: It's an interesting question!

T: Or are you saying "No, I didn't decide, they took me by force . . . they hit me." They said "You are coming with us or else . . . ?" I mean, maybe you would like to say "Look, I'm here because they picked me up and brought me here against my will . . ."

B: (Interrupts.) No, No!

T: Then? Why did you come here today?

B: Well, because I was afraid I wouldn't feel good in June.

M: By coming here, you mean?

T: Yes, by coming, And now, instead?

B: I don't feel like that any more . .

T: (Interrupts.) When they told you that we don't eat children here? . . . (Everyone laughs.)

B: (Nods.)

Actually, the therapist is metacommunicating, though very delicately, on something that is (or was) very real and dramatic for the system: The terror of going into family therapy (in fact, they are all laughing because they know it is so).

The mother then goes on to talk about the symptoms, and says that the problem resolved itself around July.

T: If I understood correctly, then, your mother is saying "In June, when there was a problem, you didn't want to come. Now that there isn't one, instead, you do come. (Everyone laughs, except Mr. Osburm.)

These remarks serve the purpose of revealing analogically the family confusion, easing the tension (which until now could be cut with a knife), and recovering neutrality.

As a matter of fact, Benjamin's problem has just reappeared with the beginning of school: He began attending classes five days after his classmates, and now still goes to school at 10 A.M. instead of 8:30. When at home, he always makes himself useful (see the first session), especially by repairing small objects (everyone in the system is visibly proud when this is mentioned). Nonetheless, Benjamin declares that as of next Monday he will resume going to school regularly ("I don't know yet if I shall be going early or late"). When the therapist questions him about the preceding session (about the fact that David might begin behaving like him), he hesitates, does not answer, and looks towards his parents; thus the information obtained is rather confused. The parents, once again, come to his rescue: "Yes, we did mention something once, but that was it."

The communication concerning the symptom seems to be calm, the designation—which was very heavy the last time—has practically disappeared, and the problem, as defined by Benjamin, is just "I don't feel like going to school."

He seems to have a marked preference for house chores: Why should he go to school, when he would much rather stay at home?

An important bit of information emerges: Mrs. Osburm, who worked nights (see the first session), has resigned and is now working in her in-laws' store (from 7:30 A.M. to 12:30 P.M. and from 5:00 P.M. to 8:00 P.M.). On Sundays the store is closed and on Saturday, when her husband is home from work, he takes care of the children and the house.

Although this unexpected decision once again causes

hypotheses on the role of the enlarged family in the family game (the store belongs to Mr. Osburm's father), it also points to the enormous changes that have taken place in the family system. For example, the possibility of a greater emphasis on the parents *as a couple*.

The therapist, naturally, must investigate the impact of this decision on the system and also on the enlarged family, in particular on Mr. Osburm's parents.

T: (To Mr. Osburm.) Were your parents pleased?

F: Well, I guess so, this decision satisfied both them and us, too.

T: It's satisfactory for you, do you mean it allows your wife to have better working hours?

F: Yes, her biorhythms are more stable, she has more time for us.

In the first session, the time factor had been used to justify, almost with the same exact words, her choosing to work at night. The therapist tries to metacommunicate on this subject.

T: More time? Well, her earlier schedule enabled her to have all afternoons free.

F: I wouldn't say that, in the morning . . . I was at the office, and the children were at school; in the afternoon, she used to sleep, so you see there wasn't really. . . .

M: (Interrupts.) Yes, and in the evening I was always in a rush because I had to leave at 10:00 P.M. . . . But then, excuse me, the important thing is that after the store closes we are all together.

Mrs. Osburm alone, at this time, emphasizes *the family reunion* as an advantage of her new job. Mr. Osburm seems to justify the decision in relation to his son's health problems, never for the whole family nor for their life as a couple.

At this time, the therapist highlights, with his easy and tranquil manner, the system's positive attitude. This very behavior is perceived as threatening by the system, which will react, as we will see, in a totally unexpected and dramatic way to this second session.

T: (Looking at Benjamin.) Mmm. What do you think about all this? Are you happy?

B: Yes, very.

T: Do you think your parents were very worried about you?

B: Yes.

T: And what about now?

B: A little less worried, I guess.

T: Do you think they are right in worrying a little less?

B: Yes.

T: Do you mean to say that those problems your Mom and Dad were so worried about last June are all gone? Do you think they worried too much?

B: Yes, I think they did.

The therapist needs to find out the *wider retroactions* to Benjamin's improvement, also because Mrs. Osburm's decision to work with her in-laws has now included once again the enlarged family.

T: (Speaking to the parents.) A few months ago, you really lived this situation dramatically didn't you?

F: Yes.

T: Hence, other people were aware of this problem. I mean, like your mother. . . .

F: Well, with regard to our family, I think I can say that everyone knew, more or less.

T: OK, but now, in your family who is aware of the changes you have made?

F: Let's say we have almost daily talks, we give them the latest developments on the problem, which in my opinion, is not completely resolved, however.

T: You mean, you think there still is a problem?

F: I mean I haven't yet understood the motives, the causes, why . . .

T: He acted this way.

It is very important that the behaviors designated as symptoms are restructured as actions or decisions; in other words, they should not be accepted passively but rather should be the outcome of a choice. In this respect, later on, the therapist makes a mistake when he says "this happened to you."

F: He had developed this . . . attitude, this refusal of school.

T: What does Benjamin say about what happened?

Benjamin says he doesn't understand either, so the therapist asks him to compile a list.

T: (To Benjamin.) In your opinion, this thing that happened to you, this refusal to go to school, who do you think understood the situation best—your mother, your father, your brother, other people who were aware of the situation?

Compiling a list is a typical informative question. If the patient is able to make the list, the therapist will have at his disposal useful information on the family coalitions; if he doesn't, as in this case, one can hypothesize that the price the patient has to pay in order to discover this difference is too high. The parents, after all, seem concerned that this difference does not emerge, so in the end the mother "helps" him by making him keep his mouth shut. Let us note the deep *lack of confirmations* Benjamin will have to suffer: He states that those *who have understood the most* are his father (who has just finished saying "he doesn't understand"), and his mother (who will in five minutes heavily disqualify him).

> **B:** (Whispers but doesn't answer.)
> **D (David):** Do you need percentages?
> **M:** (Interrupts.) No.
> **F:** (To Benjamin.) If it's someone outside the family don't be afraid to tell us.
> **B:** (To his father.) No, of course not. It's you and Joan.
> **T:** Mom and Dad, you mean. Both equally.
> **B:** Yes, yes.
> **T:** What about your mother, if we were to ask her if she has understood, would she also say, like your father: "Well, I haven't understood why he did it?" Or do you think your mother has an idea?
> **B:** I don't know.
> **M:** (Interrupts.) He has a hard time expressing himself. Even when we ask him, "Benjamin, why don't you want to go to school? Are you having problems at school, or with your classmates, are you afraid?" He always answers "I don't know. . . ."

The mother now gives a confused monologue about Benjamin, which seems to be a testimony of the deep understanding that runs between mother and son, but it ends with a disqualification.

> **M:** Maybe he sees school as an enemy, I don't know. . . . Because he says, "When I'm in the classroom I don't feel free." (Looks over at Benjamin.) What were you saying the other day? You tell me so many things that I don't even remember.

Once again, our main hypothesis has been confirmed. Benjamin does not know who his ally should be, because the messages he gets are ambiguous and each apparent confirmation is accompanied by a disconfirmation on another level.

Supervisory break. At this time, the therapist leaves to meet with his colleagues behind the one way mirror in the supervision room. The information that has emerged seems truly interesting, and differences soon arise within the therapeutic team on how the situation should be perceived. According to the therapist, the dramatization and shifting intervention has reached the system, and since in just a few months so much has changed he feels that therapy is almost over. The only real problem could be *the speed of change*, in other words, the anxiety it might cause the system. So the therapist proposes to keep the system engaged until the change has been consolidated. The supervisor, however, disagrees; he doesn't think things are going so well. Furthermore, if the system really has changed, he does not know how this change could have come about since no hypotheses on the family game were made during the last session. The supervisor also reminds the therapist of the *gravity of the problem* when it was first introduced, and highlights the father's refusal to acknowledge the change. Hence he insists on a designation. In addition, the couple has been careful not to bring up their problems. Too many dark aspects still remain. Why is the father so depressed and pessimistic now that Benjamin seems to be better? In the next half, we must try to understand. The supervisor suggests to the therapist a few questions to be asked concerning the way the family sees the future, more so than the past or present.

T: (To Benjamin.) In your opinion, are there any other problems which might worry your Mom and Dad? If your problem has gone away, or when you decide that it isn't a problem any longer, in other words—when you decide to go back to school regularly . . .

This is a typical *hypothetical question on the symptom:* "If it were to disappear, what would Mom and Dad worry about then? What would they talk about?" Invariably, the answer to this question is "Nothing," but the fact that this question has been asked cannot go unnoticed.

B: Nothing else.

T: You think, then, that if you were to go back to school normally, all the problems your Mom and Dad had with you would stop? All of them? They wouldn't have any problems? Might they not start worrying about David?

One of the fundamental rules of family therapy is "If they don't volunteer information, get it out of them any way you can" (formulate it, in other words). This statement brings to mind those lawyers in the movies who are able to make the witness say whatever they want, just by asking the right questions and suggesting the answer, at the right time, in the right way. In this case the suggestion is the shifting of the symptom. (By the end of this session, this hypothesis will have become a "reality" for the system.)

B: Yes, they might.

T: Well, what might make them worry about David?

B: If he is ill.

T: Yes, of course, but if he were not sick, what might happen to him?

B: I don't know.

T: Is there something that leads you to believe they are worried about David?

B: No, I don't think so.

The therapist then asks the children what they would like to do when they grow up. He is surprised by the fact that it is David who sees his future always at his parents' side, surrounded by his family. As a matter of fact, he would like to work with his mother in his grandparents' store.

T: (To David.) Your Mother's decision is fairly recent, isn't it? I mean to leave her old job. How did you feel about it? Were you surprised . . . was it sudden, or did you think that, sooner or later, your Mother was going to make this decision?

What the therapist is really asking is "How did your Mother's decision influence the family?" Through a series of direct and indirect questions the therapist wishes to "blame" the mother's choice for the disappearance (almost) of the symptoms, for the request for therapy, and also for the fact that Benjamin came today.

D: No, it really wasn't a surprise, because . . .

T: Had you been talking about it for a while? Did your Mom used to talk about it?

D: Yes, she talked about it sometimes.

T: In your opinion, *who was most pleased by this decision?* Make a list, excluding yourself, between your Mom, your Dad, your brother, and also other people like aunts, uncles, grandparents, and so forth. Tell me the name of the four people who were most pleased by this decision.

The therapist, once again, tries the same trick as before, the compilation of a list. Except this time with David he fares better than before. He learns a piece of very valuable information: Benjamin is very happy because his mother will spend more time at home (in fact, he feels a lot better). Our hypotheses on the *function of the symptom to bring back the mother in the family system* worked. One wonders what the father thinks, since apparently he is very unhappy (not only about his wife's decision, but also about the fact that David said so). The difference introduced by this list is a significant one. A *demarcation line* is created between the two couples, the one formed by the mother and Benjamin and the other formed by the father and David. A structural therapist would notice at once that the subsystems formed do not respect family hierarchy. What is most important, however, is that the alliances that have emerged are totally denied on a different level. The fact that they have surfaced is perceived as dangerous by the family members, particularly by the father.

D: Oh, first, my Mother . . .

T: Your Mom is the first person on the list.

D: Second is Benjamin . . .

T: Your brother is second.

D: My father is third . . . Grandma fourth and Grandpa fifth. . . .

B: (Interrupts.) I think it's Grandma and then our aunt because she works in the store, too.

D: (Tells him to shut up.) That's your opinion.

T: Your aunt, Grandma and then your aunt. . . . But you said that besides . . . ok, after your Mother, who was the first to make this decision, you said "Benjamin is second." Why?

D: Well, this way he can spend more time with her.

T: And your Dad. Isn't your Father happy that your mom . . .

D: (Interrupts.) Yes, he agrees with her decision but I think he's less happy than Mom and Benjamin.

T: Why do you think he is less happy?

F: That's right, if you made a list you must have reasoned it out.

T: That's right, so? In your opinion, why is your Dad not as happy as the others?

D: Well, he must also worry about his job. . . .

The list compiled by David is also confirmed by Benjamin. Strangely enough, Benjamin accepts the difference introduced by his brother. (We wonder: "If the therapist had asked him to compile a list, what would he have said? Would the others have let him introduce differences?")

While investigating Mrs. Osburm's decision, the therapist discovers that her husband had suggested it a long time before, but *she had always refused*, saying that she was happy with the way things were. She now feels, instead, that her new job allows her to be more serene, in addition to the advantages to her health (which she cites as the main reason behind her decision). Having asked the

mother to compile the same list, she places herself in the
first place and everyone else second.

D: I didn't think you could put everyone on the same level.
(Everyone laughs, except the father.)
T: Of course, of course! You make a list, but there's always
ex-aequo, isn't there?
D: Yes, that's what I thought. (He looks at his father.)
F: (To David, smiling.) Keep this in mind for the future.
Before you answer, always remember to ask if you can do it
ex-aequo.

This analogical exchange between David and his father
may be interpreted as an attempt on David's part to arm
himself against his father's anger (quite manifest, even on
a verbal plane).
The therapist asks Mr. Osburm the same question as
Benjamin, dealing with the *worries that might arise if the
problem were to disappear.* We are trying to see if this sudden
shift in interest from Benjamin to David is beginning to
work on the family members' premises. The father, however, still identifies the patient as Benjamin and explicitly
connects what has happened to his wife's departure. The
game is beginning to unveil itself.

F: Well, even if we do resolve this situation, in my opinion
there is still the fact that I have not yet understood what
triggered this reaction . . . this coincidence, my wife and David
going to x (name of the place), Benjamin staying with me and
from then on . . .
T: Yes.
F: Also all the repercussions this situation has had. I mean
these things, this is the first time . . . I've had to deal with
something like this; I had to put up with them, and I feel a little
. . .
T: (Interrupts.) In other words, you are saying: "I would like
to know why all this happened?"
F: Yes, exactly.

While Mr. Osburm is making these statements, his wife has assumed an expression of commiseration, intended to mean she feels differently. The therapist tries to understand the *differences between the behavior of the mother and father with regard to the problem.*

The second part of the session consists in the *building of differences* or at least in emphasizing those that have emerged. The therapist must always remain neutral: He is dealing with "differences in evaluation," and thus the differing stands are all acceptable but not "bad" or "good" per se.

T: (To the father.) It seems to me that your wife . . . she doesn't want to understand. She's merely interested in the child improving; do you think so?

F: (Interrupts.) Well, yes there is this dualism: I mean, my wife is a little . . .

T: (Interrupts to correct him.) Yes, I see, there are these *differences*, let's say, in *evaluation*.

F: Yes, exactly, she is also more optimistic, she sees things in a different light, and consequently, I guess, she's more interested in facts . . .

T: (Interrupts.) Immediate results, you mean. . . .

They continue to speak on this topic, with a slight but constant disqualification of the wife by her husband. The therapist asks Mr. Osburm what he would do if he were in his wife's shoes, and he answers by saying that he's not sure the attitude she has adopted is for the best (among other things, she frequently loses her temper, especially with the children), but for that matter neither is his.

The therapists formulate the hypothesis that the *husband is trying to make his wife feel guilty* for what has happened. After all, although Mr. Osburm openly declares his skepticism and is visibly depressed, on a relational plane it is the wife who is depressed—although she always seeks her husband's approval she is also always criticized for her optimism (which he considers superficial).

Mr. Osburm's behavior, however, can also be interpreted as mere self-pity and sense of guilt. Hence the input's indirect aim is to lift Mrs. Osburm's "down" position. Meanwhile, we underline the fact that, ideally, there might be *a connection between Benjamin's behavior and what the parents have done.*

Under the supervisor's suggestion, at the end of the session the therapist makes an input.

T: (To the mother.) The impression one gets by standing on the other side of this mirror to observe this interview, is that your husband's greater worry with respect to Benjamin's problems is partly due to the fact that he feels responsible for what happened, not because . . . of mere coincidences, in the sense that he was alone with Benjamin when the two of you left . . . and at this point the child's refusal to go to school began, maybe because he felt—this is the impression my colleagues got—this was aimed at him, that he had something to do with it. This, more or less, is the impression we got. How do you feel about this, Mrs. Osburm?

M: You mean, my husband at that time felt alone?

T: Yes, alone and thus a little guilty, and responsible too, like "you see, they go away and look at what happens, the child refuses to go to school . . . I'm not able to solve this problem."

Actually, Mrs. Osburm's response is of no consequence. The question is really an input, a veritable rereading whose purpose is to *introduce* new information and not to augment that which the therapists have already gathered.

POSTSESSION

This session has confirmed the hypothesis that Benjamin's symptoms are (or were) functional to the parents game of nondefinition of the relationship. In particular, the mother seems to be the "down" member in the parental couple, while the father seems to use Benjamin's problems to remind her of her faults. Now that Mrs. Osburm has changed her job, she seems to be better defined within the family system and Benjamin seems to have gotten back to "normal."

The therapists, however, are surprised by the father's apparent depression. They hypothesize that the shifting and dramatization intervention has ruined his chances to play his game.

In the final intervention, we shall have to lift the father, who has been penalized on various occasions, and make an intervention that positively accepts and distinguishes his worries. However, the therapeutic team seems to feel that a simple positive connotation will not suffice. Hence a paradoxical prescription will be made, instead, to give a final push to the changes that are already taking place.

Chapter 4 | THERAPEUTIC INTERVENTION

In the preceding chapters we have illustrated what goes on inside and outside the therapy room during the sessions. We shall now discuss the final moment of this encounter, the instant in which the therapist returns to the room after consulting with the observers, to discuss with the family the recommendations the group has come up with. These recommendations may be in the form of an oral or written comment (sometimes they may even be mailed at a later date if it is deemed necessary to inform an absent member).

Let us now see what happens in the here and now of a therapeutic session.

THE MAGIC OF PARADOX

The interview and the long wait that follows it contribute to increasing the expectations of the family members. We should keep in mind that they perceive and experience this situation as very serious indeed and with no apparent way out. The session has touched on painful subjects, awakened old grudges and guilt feelings. This occurs in spite of the neutral stance adopted by the therapist—a "perfect session" is after all only an ideal goal, not a realistic possibility.

It is interesting to note that pressure can sometimes be a useful tactic. At times a "soft" approach is best, but at other times the therapist will deliberately overdramatize the situation, advance a disastrous hypothesis, and openly discuss touchy family matters in order to bring about confrontation and escalation processes between family members.

We can also guess that throughout the session the members will attempt to express their requests and expectations, while avoiding as much as possible the discomforts associated with the therapeutic situation. Consequently, for our patients the therapeutic interview—on account of the topics it will inevitably deal with and most especially because of the inbred prejudices with which every family comes to the center—constitutes a new, highly restructuring experience that is also a high-strung and anxious one.

At last, after a wait of half an hour or more, the verdict arrives.

The response is not, nor does it pretend to be, binding or final, but it becomes such if we consider the situation, the involvement (including that of the therapist), and the real suffering these people are going through. And so this moment, which as we have already stated is meaningless unless the session has been conducted properly, becomes a magic moment: The "witch-doctor" therapist will now pronounce the magic formula that will make everybody happy, make life simpler, and define how everybody should behave in order for things to flow smoothly.

This personal involvement is a most natural and useful reaction since it dramatizes the impact that the session will have on the family pattern. In fact, higher expectations will be more useful the further removed they are, in context and form, from the therapeutic intervention, as we will see later on.

Unfortunately, however, this blind trust in the therapeutic intervention, especially in the use of paradoxical techniques, is not the sole prerogative of family members. Actually, it also conforms to the expectations of many a professional in the field of mental health. This attitude is becoming more and more widespread as this model of approach gains popularity; in addition, it is bringing about aberrations like inserting paradoxes at every level and in the most disparate contexts, in the erroneous conviction that this will automatically bring about a change. The literature on the subject has involuntarily augmented the blind trust in the operators, a trust which is of interest particularly to beginners who are enticed with the promise of easy success and by the more superficial aspects of paradoxical techniques.

How can this misunderstanding have started? From a careless reading of the literature on paradox and a tendency to oversimplify matters, and from a fondness on the part of several authors to focus on the more visible aspects of the therapy (which are also the easiest to explain), the miraculous insight that follows cases that turned out particularly well, and generally on the purely instrumental outlook of family therapy.

Thus for many, a systemic approach to family therapy is

identified with the use of the paradox or the therapeutic double bind and the sudden recovery of case reports; while the less flashy side—the slow and systemic construction of the object of intervention that can take place only through hypotheses and informative questions—is neglected. By now the reader should be aware that a magic intervention, a predetermined formula to be applied at will, does not exist; and more importantly, that the terms *therapy* and *intervention* are not synonymous.

The refusal to define our approach as a paradoxical therapy, however, is not solely rooted in a criticism for this kind of ready enthusiasm alone, but derives from a theoretical or epistemological criticism for the concept of paradoxicalness as the element on which the effectiveness of therapy is founded.

The question of what family therapy draws its effectiveness from has been recently spotlighted by a few authors who, like Dell, are alien to the strategic tradition.

In one of his articles, Dell (1981) defines the so-called paradoxical forms of intervention simply as nonconventional ways of carrying out therapy, thus founded on a world view different from those underlying most of the preexisting psychotherapies. He ascribes change not to paradoxicalness but to the fact that these therapists:

> Break the cultural rule according to which therapy is based on help and encouragement.

> Base their work on premises concerning the nature of human problems and their solution that the traditional approach regards as invalid (although paradox is a contradiction arising from a correct deduction and coherent premises [Watzlawick et al. 1967] that should be valid within the system at hand).

Make use of specific techniques to overcome resistance that, being perfectly consistent with their premises, are neither paradoxical nor surprising for them.

Another factor that makes it unnecessary to resort to paradoxes to explain therapeutic change is the inclusion of two fundamental parameters into therapy: time and context.

With regard to time, we know that logic is fundamentally static and that what appears paradoxical from a logical angle may not be so when an evolutionary perspective is adopted. Bateson uses the example of a buzzer circuit (1979, p. 58). The passage of current activates the electromagnet, the activated electromagnet breaks the contact, and the break in the contact deactivates the electromagnet, thus reestablishing the contact and repeating the cycle. Each of these fragments has nothing paradoxical in it, but logic, freezing the sequence, draws the conclusion that "If the contact is established, then the contact is broken," which is a real paradox, with no way out.

According to Dell (1981b) the family system may get through contradictory stages while evolving, most especially after being fed with a therapeutic input. These alternating and different stages may generate a new organization in the system, but only if we introduce the time factor. The author gives the example of the technique introduced by Selvini's group, characterized by relatively long time lapses (at least one month) between sessions as a means of allowing the system sufficient time to process an input and find a new equilibrium.

In commenting on Dell's article, Selvini has underlined the importance of context marking, which in her view renders the therapeutic intervention paradoxical by introducing unexpected information that astonishes the family, which reacts sensationally to the intervention. Hence, according to Selvini, the mainspring of change is the unexpected: People are more influenced if they expect one message and get another, on a totally different level. As a result, the premises and expectations of those taking (and not taking) part in the sessions acquire a new meaning.

This leads us to regard the effectiveness of therapy (and of intervention in particular) as founded on novelty "senso lato," rather than paradox. We will not take part in the argument on this subject between Dell and Selvini Palazzoli, limiting ourselves to joining Dell in pointing out that since systems have no expectations (which are a prerogative of individuals), they tend to react more to novelty than to unexpectedness. After all, novelty can be operatively defined only *a posteriori*, precisely in a view of the system's change (Dell 1981b, Selvini Palazzoli 1981).

On the other hand, we have already seen that family systems coming to the center are immediately confronted by novelty: novelty of the setting, of the conduct techniques, of the connections the therapist establishes between certain familial events, and of the "informative" questions.

For what reason, then, do we insist on carrying out the final intervention? What is its specific use? What are its goals?

We deem that the aim of intervention is to facilitate change. This change may variously manifest itself:

On specific behaviors (gestures, actions, symptoms).

On rules and patterns (behavior sequences, relationships, escalations).

On the premises (system's epistemology, myths, hypotheses on the problem).

These elements are all connected, and the change that takes place in one drags out changes in the others. But ultimately we place emphasis on premises precisely because they represent the most general context, which frames and gives meaning to the first two. The premises represent the intervention's "metagoal," the privileged object of change. Consequently, it is impossible to make an intervention that is disconnected from the tracking done during the session: There must be an ultimate consistency between all phases of teamwork. One of the founding principles of the Palo Alto group—which first introduced "brief therapy," stating "first change, then understand" (Watzlawick et al. 1967, 1974, Weeks and L'Abate 1982) is debatable. Therapeutic change is a question of learning and thus cannot prescind from meanings.

We have just seen that no ready-made formulas for the construction of an effective therapeutic intervention exist. Strategic therapists generally establish a link between the goal and the intervention strategies; as a result, once the real problem is singled out, intermediate goals can be fixed for the purpose of hitting just that pattern. The evaluation should be automatic: Either the goal is achieved or it is not.

In our model everything is less finalized, less predetermined (MacKinnon 1983). This is not so much a shortcoming in the model as a precise choice for favoring, once again, autonomy and underlining the unity of the families that come to us for help. The implicit premise is that the system will not do anything it could not have done by itself. From our point of view, the therapeutic team's job is neither that of witch doctor nor codifier (planner); rather, the team behaves like a catalyst of the natural process of change. The two systems meeting both change, at least to a certain extent.

FUNCTIONS AND CHARACTERISTICS OF SYSTEMIC INTERVENTION

We have stated that intervention and interview share the same object; hence it is important that they be consistent. In our model, the intervention is structured as a recapitulation of the elements that have emerged during the interview. The intervention highlights, albeit often only indirectly, the connections the conduct techniques have revealed; it strengthens the problem's alternative punctuations; and it introduces the team's hypotheses. Furthermore, it paves the way for the following interview and makes it more fruitful, thus ensuring a link for the continuation of therapy. (One may also say that the session constitutes a preparatory work for the intervention, and thus the chain is complete.)

It follows that we can list numerous functions that the paradoxical (or nonparadoxical) intervention carries out simultaneously. The intervention:

1. Emphasizes the existence of a therapeutic context.
2. Entails the system's active involvement in the therapeutic work.
3. Promotes informative retroactions (on both the system's engagement into therapy and the family rules).
4. Identifies the boundaries of the system or subsystem involved and the set of relationships on which the therapist has decided to focus in order to ensure change.

5. Provides a structure for subsequent interventions and sessions (this also means that every intervention somehow limits future resources, since it operates as a selection).

The team carries out all of these functions, plotting interventions consistent with the model—informative (plausible-unexpected), circular, and neutral.

THE INTERVENTION AS A CHALLENGE TO EPISTEMOLOGICAL PREMISES

As far as the *plausibility* of the intervention is concerned, we will refer to what we have already said in Chapter 3: It is impossible to make oneself intelligible to anyone unless one uses the same language. The systemic intervention takes shape in accordance with the information provided by the system and by those rare occasions on which the therapist introduces some entirely arbitrary punctuations (such as the dramatization and shifting intervention in our clinical case's first session) because the session has been scarcely informative and has not achieved its goals. An implausible final intervention could nullify the benefits of a well-conducted session for it reintroduces the confusion, the disqualification of the therapist, as well as the manipulation of information. We are now most concerned, however, in determining how, after an ideal interview, to construct an unexpected intervention, one that defies the family's premises.

The extent to which the intervention is unexpected depends on the domain in which it will operate; in the first place, one must consider how the family system arrives to therapy.

The path is of a random and unpredictable character. Above all, one thing is evident: The link between disturbance and request for therapy must not be taken for granted—a mental disorder does not automatically lead to therapy, and the request for therapy does not always indicate the *presence* of psychiatric problems. In the first place, a preliminary selection takes place between the systems (and the individuals) who are candidates for therapy: The perception of the disorder, as well as its definition as a psychological disorder, is connected to many and various occasions, social and cultural factors, external interferences, and so forth. Second, every system can find by itself the solution to its own problems, however unorthodox in the eyes of the expert this solution may appear.

In our field, the study of spontaneous change has proved particularly useful; it seems to appear in those situations where new events cannot be framed within a preexisting world view. The request for therapy itself may be considered an opportunity to accumulate experience, to mature. In this case, the term *learning* (in a Batesonian sense) seems to be more apt than the traditional and rather vague *change*.

Therefore, if professional intervention is requested, it is because a problem exists, but perhaps also because the premises do not work—they cannot embrace the whole reality and point out the solutions required along the way.

Hence the system calls for help. One may think, at this point, that it feels in danger and the request for outside intervention acts as a "search for equilibrium."

How can such a search for equilibrium be reconciled with change? This is a typical "pseudo-problem"[1] to which many have endeavored to work out an answer:

_____

[1]We call it a "pseudo-problem" because it seems clear that the problem lies precisely with the identification of this "search for equilibrium" with a search for "that particular equilibrium"—namely, the "status quo." Actually it is always a "new equilibrium" (Dell 1982, Elkaim 1981).

"Do families want to change or don't they?" One of the first observations put forward by family therapists (in accordance with the family homeostasis hypothesis described in Chapter 1) was that the messages of the family members presented some discrepancies between the verbal-explicit and the analogical-implicit levels. On a verbal level, the message was: "We want to change" (although this change referred to personal problems, to the symptom, or to domains so vaguely defined as to be indeterminable). On the other hand, the analogical message associated with such a request was often disqualifying toward the therapeutic context, or revealed rejection or confusion with regard to the presentation of the system's expectations. In short, according to this interpretation families would try communicating in thousands of ways that "We are not here to change." These observations prompted the Milan group to give preference to the hypothesis—provocative and useful at the same time[2]— according to which the system arrives to therapy not when the symptom or the problem reaches its zenith but rather when the change is already in progress and everybody is scared by it. Besides, this hypothesis does not appear so absurd as it may seem at first when one notes that the system often resorts to therapy only when the symptom has been in existence for years and is already declining or has even disappeared.

Since we are talking about provocations: What is the therapist's ultimate task but to put an end to the request for therapy? The ultimate goal of the therapeutic process is not an improvement in the patient or a real and

---

[2]Its usefulness probably derives precisely from the defiance to the traditional, or more obvious, premises. Thus the challenge, the provocation, not only "changes the system" but also, and most especially, it changes the scientific community, the stale models on which psychiatry is founded, the clichés, and so forth.

substantial change in the family's patterns. It is precisely the end of the request for therapy that indicates to the therapist that his job is over.

Once again we must take into account the system's premises and epistemology. The request for therapy is part of the very premises from which the problem has arisen. When the premises change and the system is able to contrive new solutions, it suddenly perceives the uselessness of therapy, and leaves. The so-called "therapeutic dropout" is from a theoretical point of view the ideal conclusion of a therapeutic relationship, since it shows the system has acquired greater autonomy (all this in defiance of any idea of control of the process on the part of the therapist).

Getting back to the issue of the system's "condition," we feel that a correct approach to the whole question, according to our theory of change, could be to view the system requesting therapy as one that has come to a deadlock and requires a fresh input to start it up again. With regard to novelty, Selvini Palazzoli states that a foreseeable intervention is ineffective, while Dell would say that an intervention is "coherent" or "incoherent" with the system rather than "foreseeable" or "unforeseeable" (Dell 1981a, Selvini Palazzoli 1981).

From a practical point of view, challenging the system's epistemological premises means never providing it with what is expected. In this respect, the most appropriate answer to a request for therapy, for instance, would be a refusal to grant therapy.

Similarly, the use of such an intervention as the *prescription of the symptom* is fully justifiable: The system's request, over and beyond its being a true double bind, is for a change in the problematic behavior; therefore the therapists are expected to act restrictively. What a surprise for family members when they are told that for the time being this behavior is useful and every endeavor should be made not to alter it! Even more surprising would be the reason the therapeutic team gives them for this prescription (the positive connotation), a reason contrary to every sensible expectation.

Another element of novelty in the therapeutic intervention pertains to the analogical plane: If the family behaves lightly and in a fatuous manner the therapist often introduces a dramatic intervention, puts forward tragic hypotheses about the future, and suggests that aggravations or accidents might occur. If, on the other hand, the atmosphere of the session is particularly grave and the weight of the identification is entirely felt, the problem will be minimized or shifted toward someone else during the intervention, or the therapist will insinuate doubts on other domains the system had "dismissed" as nonproblematic. Those behaviors *defying the rules of therapy* (dropouts, delays, interruptions during the session, absences and so on) will accordingly be *"reinforced"* (the word appears in quotations since the effect, in this case, is chiefly inhibiting rather than strengthening).

In this respect, a dangerous domain is one that embraces the patients' expectations with regard to values: Obviously they expect negative judgments, advice, accusations, just as they make themselves. But now we are straying into the subject of neutrality, which we will deal with later on.

THE INTERVENTION'S CIRCULARITY AND NEUTRALITY

With regard to the circularity and neutrality of the systemic intervention, we do not have much to add to what we said in Chapter 3 concerning the conduct of the session. Intervention and session, in fact, cannot but be contingent. What do we mean when we affirm that the intervention must be a "circular" or, better, a "total" one? The comments, restructurings, and prescriptions that make up the intervention, the convocation itself of the system or part of it to a few family therapy sessions, always carry with them the danger of a loss of balance. Every time one provides a partial (or biased) punctuation one indirectly emphasizes the causative role of a particular family member in the insurgence or persistence of the problem. In particular, it is easy to regard the patient as a powerless member and consequently to structure the intervention so as to relieve the burden of the identification, possibly at the expense of other members.

It is precisely for these reasons that the intervention must be carefully devised. The prescription of the symptom is coupled with a prescription for the others or a comment embracing the whole system. In a few cases an acknowledgement of each member's effort, attention, or contribution can precede the intervention. In this way, everyone feels involved.

These observations refer back to those we made earlier on neutrality: Just like the interview, the intervention must be positive and must not induce any feelings of guilt or implicitly suggest to either the system or one of its members that it is wrong.

If one regards the interview as a premise for the intervention, the neutrality of the latter should not be difficult to attain: One can hypothesize that the family's perception of the context, after a one-hour session, is that of a neutral situation where there is no point in playing the moralist, where every idea is accepted for what it is, and where no hostile coalitions are allowed. Such perceptions help bring about both change and involvement.

In summary, the intervention's neutrality and circularity can once more be included in the more general subject of novelty of therapy. Neutrality in particular is an element of novelty significantly affecting the family's premises, patterns, and different behaviors. The wisdom we have frequently mentioned has positive effects on those situations characterized by guilt feelings, fragmentation, and identification with which the systems arrive to therapy. This is consistent with our idea of therapy—that it should not only provide new models that make the symptom unnecessary but also strengthen the system's autonomy, driving it towards an increased flexibility and adaptability.

The example that most clearly illustrates these concepts is the one provided by those systems arriving at our center with an endless record of diagnoses, interviews, and therapies. The situation for such families has crystallized in a recursive sequence: distress, request for therapy, disqualification of the therapist, dropping out, distress. Such systems progressively isolate themselves, becoming increasingly shrewd and determined. They come to the center with definite expectations about what we will do and say. In these cases, our hypothesis is that the true problem lies with the request for therapy and that complying with the system's requests would imply certain failure. This is one of those situations where our technique proves particularly fruitful since, unlike other forms of therapy that act on a single plane and generally pertain to contents and verbal expressions, it works on all levels of communication. It accepts the family into therapy while qualifying the context as a nontherapeutic one, or states that therapy cannot be undertaken while at the same time calling a meeting with all of the members. This is a paradoxical way to break the vicious circle, as it prevents the double bind implicit in their message "We are in therapy, but we are not" simply by anticipating it.

In such cases any further intervention may prove unnecessary. Once the relationship is defined, things seem to straighten themselves out.

To end with, let us consider another paradigmatic case: the family with no therapeutic record, no designation, and no definite expectations. In this case, the therapist's skill may prevent the system from taking the usual course and help it in finding alternative solutions to therapy. Since the problem is still in an emerging stage, one is free to interpret, shift, and redefine it in thousands of alternative ways, rather than merely attributing a diagnostic label ascribing blame and responsibilities or strictly adhering to social and cultural rules.

These two cases may appear antithetic, but both require that the work should be carried out almost exclusively on the context and call for practically no intervention at all, at least in the classic sense of the term. Such are the cases that make our approach a "nontherapy" or maybe even a "metatherapy"; our method, in fact, may appear more as a technique of intervention on the faults of therapy rather than a particular type of treatment.

INTERVENTION TECHNIQUES: A GENERALIZATION

If generalizing is always difficult in family therapy, it is particularly so with regard to the intervention, since each intervention is a whole, unique in its line, whose parts all have a raison d'être—at least in reference to those perfect and very rare interventions.

The systemic intervention is by definition something complex. Some interventions are remarkably long and involve restructurings, positive connotations, assignments, and metaphors, while others are apparently simpler (although a single comment or a convocation for an interview may conceal an unimaginable multiplicity of codification levels).

One reason for this complexity lies in the fact that, like all communications, it includes two different kinds of messages, a verbal-explicit and an analogical-implicit one. Furthermore, several relationships are defined at the same time: between the therapist and the system (or one of its members), between the therapeutic system and the wider institutional context, between the present company and the absent figures.

We have decided to classify the different parts of the intervention into three main groups on the basis of their form and their privileged target. Each of the techniques singled out may be regarded as an intervention per se or as an element concurring in granting various functions at the same time: neutrality, engagement of the family, definition of the problem and of the goals of the session, and correction of the inevitable blunders and errors that are made in the conduct of the sessions. The intervention techniques we will describe are restructuring, the simple prescription, and the metaphoric prescription.

RESTRUCTURING

Restructuring more or less directly affects the interpretations and thus the world view (at least of the problem illustrated), the premises, and the beliefs that have originated the identification and led to therapy. Restructuring may be defined as a "reelaboration of different relational schemes through the use of preexisting elements" (Andolfi 1979, Watzlawick et al. 1974). In other words, the same basic building blocks are used but they are arranged differently. Restructuring's potential for change springs from the principle according to which if a new game is introduced the system will not be able to view things from the same angle as before and thus to play the old game (Wittgenstein 1956).

According to its contents restructuring may acquire different denominations: rereading, alternative punctuation, redefinition, contextual resetting, as well as shifting, paradoxical interpretation, prescription, and so on. Numerous authors regard restructuring more as a branch category rather than an intervention per se: All interventions are restructuring, though at different levels (behavioral, contextual, semantic, etc.).

A particular restructuring technique developed by the Milan group is the *positive connotation* of all family member's behaviors (Selvini Palazzoli et al. 1978). The positive connotation, in addition to carrying out the functions generally granted by all interventions, answers to a few particular needs (Selvini Palazzoli et al. 1978). These needs are to:

1. Put everybody on the same level (neutrality). First effect: relief from the weight of identification and removal of individual feelings of guilt.
2. Introduce an element of novelty into the expectations: They expect a negative judgment and are, instead, ascribed the noblest of intentions.
3. Enter into an alliance with the system, accepting its good intentions and goals. In this respect, it strengthens the therapeutic relationship (neutrality again, but this time toward the whole system rather than single members).
4. Provide a good reason for accepting the prescription (the symptom/behavior of X is "good," thus stay like this). "Evil" cannot be prescribed. If we want to talk about paradoxicalness, the positive connotation is paradoxical in itself, even without a prescription. The message is: "What we are here

to change is intrinsically good," but why should
something so noble and generous give birth to a
pathology?
5. Define the therapist as "one-up" with respect to
the system, and at any rate propose a relationship
in respect to which family members cannot fail to
define themselves.

It is important to point out that the positive connotation is
not a trick contrived to deceive the system; on the
contrary, it further confirms that the team has acquired a
real circular and neutral attitude of mind (Bateson's "wisdom"): Who feels they have the right to criticize the
system? At each moment the system is as is and has to be
taken as such and not for "what it should be if it were not
like this."

The restructuring can also take place through some
metaphorical rereading of the evidence emerged during
the interview. When faced with the residue of a problem,
for example, one may draw a parallel with the scars left by
a surgical operation: The scars are there to witness the
disappearance of the illness, but cannot be eliminated and
one must learn to live with them.

Those interpretations that completely distort the system's punctuations are additional examples of restructuring: They shift the problem from the patient to other
members of the system, reinterpret the deprecated behaviors on a different key, and derive new meanings from the
old behaviors.

Restructuring seems to let in by the back door a concept
that the authors of *Pragmatics of Human Communication*
(Watzlawick et al. 1967) had banned: "insight." The
interpretations (or better readings) the therapist puts forth
in family therapy, however, are not aimed at increasing
people's awareness of their own problems, but rather at

having them experience a new situation (or a new and different outlook on the same situation, which is ultimately the same). An alternative way to outline the terms of the problem is to affirm that to unveil the game to the system is quite a different matter than to unveil it to single members. In our case, it is the system that becomes aware, if one can talk about awareness. Unlike more normative theories and therapies, the final outcome of family therapy as we conceive it should not be a more accurate knowledge of the problem but precisely the idea that no absolute map exists. In other words, therapeutic experience should result in an increased flexibility of the system—that is, it should lead to the Learning II level.

THE SIMPLE PRESCRIPTION

A "classical" intervention technique that has characterized this form of therapy from the very beginning is the *paradoxical prescription*, otherwise known as *illusion of alternatives* (Watzlawick et al. 1967, Andolfi 1979, Hoffman 1981, and Selvini Palazzoli et al. 1978). This is the typical situation where the family system, whatever its response, "plays the therapist's game." Although restructuring has ideas as its target, the prescription acts primarily at a pragmatic level, and thus it is the aspect of therapy closest to the guidelines set by the authors of the systemic approach. The therapeutic double bind, the therapeutic paradox, and the "counterparadox" of the Milan group share the same basic idea of having the family actually experience a new situation, which also has no way out, but this time in an "adaptational" sense. To quote *Pragmatics of Human Communication:* "Prescribing the symptom is only one of the many and various paradoxical interventions which can be classified as double binds . . . *Similia similibus curantur*, in other words those situations that, according to research, lead people to madness must eventually be used to make them sane again."

Again from *Pragmatics*:

On a structural plane the therapeutic double bind is the reflexed image of the pathogenic one:

1. It implies an intense relationship—in this particular instance, the psychotherapeutic situation—from which the patient expects a reason to live.
2. In this context an injunction is made so as to (a) strengthen the behavior the patient expects to be changed, (b) imply that such a reinforcement can bring about a change, and thus (c) create the paradox, since the patient is invited to change while remaining as he/she is.
3. The therapeutic situation prevents the patient from withdrawing into himself/herself or otherwise dissolving the paradox by commenting on it.

Since it is a behavioral indication, it proves more efficient than any criticism or correction also because the affirmative form ("Do this and that") has a stronger hold than the negative one ("Stop behaving this way").

Even if today, as we have seen, one wonders whether these techniques are really paradoxical and whether it still makes sense to talk of therapeutic double bind, it cannot be denied that such interventions are so effective that they give rise to enormous expectations. Besides, it is precisely the "miraculous" paradoxical prescription that has aroused a great interest in family therapy. Several types of therapeutic intervention, even not strictly within family or systemic therapy, are based on the principles of paradoxical prescription. Let us see, however, what this means. When facing a problem, one generally tends to do the most logical thing to solve it. In psychotherapy, however, what is logical seldom works; on the contrary, it often adds to the problem (Watzlawick et al. 1974); besides, if that were the right path toward a solution, the system would already have taken it by itself. Instead, all obvious solutions have clearly failed and the system asks for therapy implicitly believing that the therapist will propose some equally obvious—and thus ineffective—solutions.

The paradoxical approach to therapy affirms that a way to influence symptoms is to have them voluntarily put into being. By definition, a prescribed behavior cannot be spontaneous, thus losing the particular distinction of symptoms, uncontrollability. This does not only apply to behaviors with a psychiatric label, but also to single actions, sequences of actions, and entire family patterns, that can also be prescribed. Such a prescription leaves the system no choice: If they comply with it, they perform a voluntary deed, and they obey the therapist, thus ratifying the context of change. If they do not comply, they drop the symptom or the dysfunctional behaviors prescribed, and change. In both cases the intervention's aims are achieved. To be effective, however, prescriptions must be accurately planned so as to leave no chance for escape through a disqualification or a new counterparadox.

Actually, a paradoxical prescription could also be avoided in a sane manner through metacommunication. As we have pointed out, however, this is a way out that is available to our families, since their communications are so confused and ambiguous that any comment regarding the relationship becomes impossible: Metacommunicating implies the ability to clearly define the relationship both on a verbal and an analogical level, thus making the symptom unnecessary. It is generally regarded as a sign of good health, and the observation that the more serious the disorder the smaller the capacity to metacommunicate corroborates this hypothesis.

Even the convocation of the system into therapy may become a paradoxical prescription. The message "you are in therapy" that is implicit in the convocation of the family is often coupled with a comment such as "therapy is not necessary" or "family therapy would be advisable, but dangerous."

The same effect is obtained by splitting up the system, especially if it takes place at an early stage: "Family therapy is advisable in your case, so we have decided to meet with just the parents on this date. . . ." In this case, a redefinition of the boundaries and relations between subsystems is added to the prescription.

The paradox can be used to ensure the engagement of the system or the therapeutic relationship. An example of this technique is provided by what Watzlawick calls "use of resistance " (Watzlawick et al. 1974), namely, the prescription of resistance as a condition for change. Opposing change has proved an extremely useful technique when used with the so-called therapist-killers, those families that bump off (in a metaphorical sense, of course) one therapist after another. Such systems have enough experience to expect that the therapist will desire, request, and even demand change (at whatever level it is to take place). Consequently, they are astonished by the family therapist's request: "Please, don't change, not just yet," or "It could be very dangerous for X" or "for therapy" or "for the whole family unit." A similar effect is achieved by "restraining" change: "Try not to change too quickly." Such a prescription suggests that change is taken for granted. Besides, this is not far from what the therapist actually thinks; according to the theory of equilibrium too sudden a change may bring about a destablization in the system, which could react with a relapse—never by slipping back to the status quo—and thus is not desirable.

Paradoxical therapists classify prescriptions into two categories: those aimed at obtaining the patients' compliance and those whose goal is disobedience, dropping out, or the remission of the symptom (Weeks and L'Abate 1982).

If we consider the epistemological premises on which our model is based, and the concept of information in particular, a classification such as the one listed above makes little sense. Intervention is communication, and as such it never fails to bring about a response from the system and its components. Wondering which should be the most desirable response—compliance or disobedience—also does not make sense, since every response is (or must be) foreseen and at any rate carries with it some information essential for the continuation of therapy, regardless of its being expected or even induced by the therapeutic team. The mere fact that a prescription has been made, in fact, entails a change in the context of the prescribed behaviors. Hence, we would like to reaffirm a concept already introduced with reference to therapeutic hypotheses: What family therapists attach great importance to is not a complete disappearance of the symptoms, possible at the very first session and with no subsequent relapses, but rather that any improvement, worsening, or even stationary state of the dysfunctional behaviors should be framed within the hypothesis and receive an adequate response from the team. The response depends on the situation, context, preceding interventions, stage of the therapeutic intervention, and so on. In summary, the prescription's specific purposes are to:

1. Mark the therapeutic context.
2. Induce a retroaction in the family, enlightening their

availability and motivation to a possible treatment.
3. Outline the area under study.
4. Structure and regulate the following sessions (Selvini Palazzoli et al. 1978).

Point 1 is common to all types of intervention. It confirms the therapist's position, which is generally strengthened by the positive connotation.

Point 2 affirms that the prescription is a test providing information on the system's engagement, in addition to the information concerning the validity of the hypothesis.

Point 3 refers to the system or subsystem at which the prescription is aimed (for instance, the parents or the children); to the prescription's power to draw boundaries within the system itself; and to larger systems such as those comprising the family of origin. Moreover, the choice of a particular content emphasizes a precise area of troublesome relationships, not necessarily the one the family considers to be the problem.

Finally, point 4 places the session on a specific plane: Every meeting with the family should comprise a few questions on the previous session's intervention. This is an extremely important verification of the hypotheses on which that session was founded. Furthermore, it is a familiar topic that everyone will be able to discuss and an ideal starting point for gathering additional information.

THE METAPHORICAL PRESCRIPTION

The term *metaphorical prescription* (Andolfi 1979) is somewhat ambiguous. It does not refer to a supposed metaphorical characteristic of the intervention but rather to the fact that the behaviors prescribed are not directly linked to the problem presented, which are thus regarded as metaphors of the target behaviors.

The target of this type of intervention is neither the system's ideas nor its behaviors, but rather the context. Once again we have a restructuring effect, but in this case through an analogical mechanism. In the ritual, and partly in the assignment, all the gestures, contexts, sequences of actions, as well as the latter's rhythm, are crystallized by strict programming and introduced into the system as a constant (Selvini Palazzoli 1978a, Selvini Palazzoli et al. 1977a, 1978).

This type of prescription needs neither interpretations norcomments, and is particularly apt for those families that have problems in expressing themselves verbally or, at the other extreme, for those that are particularly skillful at manipulating oral communication. No metacommunication, in fact, is required here; what is required instead is to act *together* and *for a common purpose*.

Under this category we have included all those prescriptions aimed at attaining change through the execution of a task to be performed jointly—namely assignments and rituals. The difference between these two interventions is quite a subtle one and rests not so much on the substance as on the emphasis placed on some particular aspects. Generally speaking, assignments are less structured and strict and may involve only part of the system (possibly with a prescription of silence toward the others). The characteristics of these interventions are totality, planning, and external leadership.

TOTALITY

More so than other types of intervention, ritual is able to guarantee circularity and to take into account all the behavior of all the members of the system, since everyone is assigned a particular role. The feeling of belonging is thus emphasized and consequently, in addition to circularity, neutrality is also guaranteed.

PLANNING

Each metaphorical prescription (rituals, as we have seen, more so than others) qualifies various and numerous aspects: actions and gestures, words, contexts, as well as when and how often it will have to be implemented. This means that each family member, at a given moment determined in advance, will carry out a specific task and that this very task will be repeated at a given frequency, in the interval between the two sessions. Little space is left to chance, self-determination, and individual decisions, at least with regard to those aspects deemed important for the effectiveness of the ritual.

EXTERNAL LEADERSHIP

The therapist decides all of this and requires that everything be done as agreed, without comment (quite often this is a very relevant feature of prescription). This circumstance frees the family members from all responsibility, since no one must be responsible for the others' actions, no one plays the controller (if someone is given this role it is within the scope of the prescription and thus under the therapist's "metacontrol"), and no one must conceive meanings and attributions (all meanings have been previously assigned by the therapist's intervention). As a result, the system's members, at least for a short while, play a game that is different from the usual one and are able to apply the metaphor ("It is as if we were like this . . .") to themselves. Such an experience paves the way for change, or at least introduces the idea that a change is possible.

Metaphorical prescriptions may vary. Each case is unique and the contrivance of a task or a ritual requires imagination on the part of the therapeutic team, in addition to its ability to read the family's "culture" and to single out its salient features. Thus there are simple assignments, possible for parents only, that are implemented just once, such as an evening outing without the children having knowledge of it. There are recurrent assignments, where there is someone who does something with someone else, someone who makes sure that this something is actually done, and possibly even someone whose task is to remind the former "to do" and the latter "to make sure." Finally, there are true rituals. As defined by the Milan group, a ritual is "an action or a series of actions, usually combined with verbal phrases and expressions into which all family members are called on to take part. In fact, to be effective rituals must involve the whole family" (Selvini Palazzoli et al. 1978).

Besides, it is precisely for this reason that rituals are remarkably difficult prescriptions and that assignments, which have less dramatic force, are more frequent.

What accounts for the effectiveness of ritualized prescriptions? We can list at least five specific functions.

1. They give persons who have lost all hope of resolving the problem the opportunity of experiencing an operative situation. Moreover, they provide new and more functional relational models.
2. They delimit a system (or subsystem); doing something together, in fact, creates a group and separates its members from the others, drawing boundaries. The *splitting* it creates can be strengthened by a prescription of silence.
3. They extend the therapeutic process. With both the ritual and the assignment the system "takes the therapist home with it," availing itself of the learning opportunities afforded by the therapeutic context. Hence it becomes unnecessary to meet

with the family frequently; on the contrary, the longer the family is left to freely process inputs, the more autonomous, active, and thus from our point of view sane, the process of change will be.

4. They indirectly emphasize some new aspects of the family's situation, adaptational meanings attributable to the problem behaviors, reciprocal cause and effect relations between the problems and the solutions already experimented, and vicious circles within the family's relationships. An "on the field" restructuring takes place that blocks (at least in some circumscribed situations) the system's dysfunctional behaviors—denied coalitions, exploitations, secrets, and so on.

5. They enable the gathering of relational information. The fact that all the members participate in the assigned tasks means that a few triadic questions on the execution of the respective assignment can be asked in the next session, opening up the possibility of pointing out differences.

THE INTERVENTION–HYPOTHESIS RELATIONS

In Chapter 2, dealing with therapeutic hypotheses, we tried to approach clinical science with a measure of scientific rigor. This led us to break down therapy into three phases that highlight the scientific sequence that hypotheses undergo while the work with the family proceeds.

1. In the first phase, data and information come together in a series of hypotheses, with which the

therapists endeavor to frame the symptom in a significant structure. These hypotheses emphasize the privileged relationships and coalitions, place the members of the system into triadic relations, and on a metalevel link family and therapist in a single larger system.

2. The information that has emerged during the sessions makes a choice possible: A few plausible and unexpected hypotheses are introduced in the family system members' world view through conduct techniques.

3. Lastly, the intervention is constructed on the area of relationships that have shown to be the most directly linked to the problem illustrated.

This last phase constitutes a real check on the hypotheses. The end-of-the-session intervention is "intrinsically a trial, an input in the system that *cannot fail* to bring about an output (either immediately or after a short while), some sort of clarifying retroaction. As a result, the retroactions will serve as control mechanisms for the therapists' hypotheses. Should an hypothesis prove incorrect, a new one will have to be formulated" (Selvini Palazzoli et al. 1977b).

Such a verification, however, will be only an indirect one since the hypothesis is not entirely and automatically incorporated into the intervention. The conclusions to be given to the family must in fact be comprehensible, formulated in a language able to provide some alternative punctuation while remaining linear.

The relation between the intervention and the hypothesis underlying it is very much like that between analogical and numerical communication. In fact, although the hypothesis explicates and rationalizes the game, the session's final conclusions reveal it though they do not interpret or verbalize it, nor explicitly state that it has to be changed. On the contrary, we have seen that their effectiveness has been connected precisely to the fact that they side with the game, that they are "homeostatic" (though on a different plane, highly antihomeostatic, circularizing and autonomizing for the system).

The fact that we consider a successful intervention as an indirect confirmation of the hypothesis, is tied to the observation that the hypothesizing activity alone provides those items of information that one must avail oneself of to work successfully on levels of communication. This observation is also valid for those interventions that do not work: Only the formulation of precise working hypotheses enables it to fully comprehend the failure and turns it into a useful source of information for the continuance of therapy.

For this reason, postsession hypotheses are slightly different from the preceding ones, being functional to the intervention. An attempt is made to foresee the system's reactions to the "proposal of relationship" arising from the intervention (e.g., a possible disqualification) so as to prevent them. An attempt is made to make the prescription plausible and acceptable and to repair the cracks and shifts that may have formed during the session. Consequently, during the team discussion a series of intervention proposals are gradually discarded on the ground that though theoretically correct and coherent with the triadic hypotheses, they entail scarcely informative retroactions from the family[3] or a too sudden, and thus dangerous, change or disqualification of the therapeutic context. (An additional danger may consist in a self-disqualification

---

[3]An ideal intervention is one that leaves no alternatives or way out. Unexpected responses create problems in the formulation of hypotheses that frame and provide them with meaning.

deriving from interventions that were not coherent with the definition given in the context, such as therapeutic interventions in a nontherapeutic context.)

In short, after the therapeutic relationship has been granted an *adequate context*, after a technically correct and *informative session* has been conducted and *plausible and useful hypotheses conducive to change (namely new ones)* have been formulated, the final intervention must above all be constructed in view of the strategic requirements of therapy as well as the *treatment plan*. Only thus can the two aspects of clinical work, the cognitive-diagnostic and the resolutive-restructuring one, be integrated.

CLINICAL CASE: THERAPEUTIC MOVES

In this section we resume the case study that we have followed in Chapters 2 and 3.

THE PARADOXICAL PRESCRIPTION IN THE SECOND SESSION

At the conclusion of the second session, the therapist gave the following conclusions to the Osburm family:

As you recall, last time we merely familiarized ourselves with your family situation. We told you that, on the basis of our experience and the information gathered, we were more worried for David than for Benjamin. We also told you that this remark was based on our firsthand experience with similar cases, case-reports from other family therapy centers like ours, statistics, and typologies, You are a prototype family composed of four persons, with two male brothers of only a few years' age difference. Thus it appeared to us that David might also be in danger. For this reason, we told you: "Let us meet again to verify this possibility, but most of all, for a veritable consultation session so that we can dissolve the prognosis as well as solve the diagnostic question." Our problem was mainly to figure out the problem; once we knew that, we could decide what to do. We would now like to tell you that this session has provided us with all the information we needed to be absolutely certain about what we told you the last time, in other words, we are most concerned that Benjamin's problem might, somehow, be transferred to . . . It's a little like metastasis: Once a tumor is removed from the organism, there is the risk of it transferring to another part of the body. Experience has taught us that, though we don't know how this happens, it almost inevitably does occur.

Hence, today we reaffirm that your family typology is of this kind and that we are very worried about David.

What we can do, in this case, is to continue our meetings in the hope that we might discover the mechanism through which this might take place, thus to perform what we call prevention work with respect to this possibility, which though very high might also not take place after all.

However, we only ask one thing. What we are about to do, and in part are already doing, is a bit like enlarging the negative of a picture; hence, you must think of yourselves as a picture which we wish to enlarge in order to study it more carefully. It is very important for us that the negative be as identical as possible to the preceding one, in other words if the negative changes each time we study it, we risk losing a lot of time and making our task much harder. Therefore, we have decided to see you again in 45 days, but we ask that until then you remain as much as possible as we have seen you today.

I shall be even more precise: with regard to Benjamin, if it were possible for him to continue going to school between 9:30–10:00 A.M. instead of 8:00 A.M. for the rest of the month it would mean a lot to us. Now, we realize we might be asking the impossible. . . . Let us say this would satisfy our highest desire. Our highest desire is that the family remain absolutely identical. For this reason, it would be propitious for Benjamin to try as hard as he can to stay at home on Monday, instead of going to school like he had planned. Of course, only if he wants to, but you should know that any change in your present situation makes our work a little harder. We realize this might seem very inconsequential, but to us it is very important.

Having cleared this up, we would like you to know that next time we plan on continuing our analysis, our enlargement. As your husband (looking over to Mrs. Osburm) rightfully said, "After all, I am worried not so much for what is happening right now, as for the fact that I don't understand . . . "and he is perfectly right, in the sense that our biggest problem is not to highlight a good, positive, and calm situation as much as to understand what triggered the initial problem, because when these symptoms are transmitted they grow in intensity, so if Benjamin was, on a scale from 1 to 10, a 2, David will be a 4.

This intervention may be subdivided into two parts. The *first part*, with regard to content, is a mere repetition of what had been said at the end of the preceding session, which we had defined as "a dramatization and shifting intervention on the symptom" (this technique falls in the restructuring category).

The immediate aim of that intervention had been to lighten the patient's role without playing the problem down (otherwise this might bring about a sudden symmetric escalation and consequently the loss of the therapeutic relationship). A bigger aim was to redefine the problem as a mere family problem (this redefinition, as we shall see, will be slowly constructed throughout the therapeutic process); as soon as David gets involved, the problem ceases to be individual.

From a technical standpoint, the first session's intervention had been a veritable bluff. Usually each content given in the conclusion is made plausible through the construction of ideas during the session, is anticipated in the questions, and is justified by the information given. In this case, however, the situation was totally different because the family had not provided the therapist with information and he, in turn, had not actively constructed any.

Hence, shifting the symptom to David might then be considered a mere attempt. It is even more surprising in view of its immediate effectiveness in bringing Benjamin to the session.

In the conclusions to the second session, what we see is apparently the same intervention. The context in which it takes place, however, is totally different: The retroaction to the preceding session has been good, and one may therefore consider that the idea suggested by the therapist is now part of their premises and has begun to work as such. Furthermore, we have new information concerning the father's behavior towards change, the mother's role within the system, and so forth. Actually, dramatizing the problem would now become a *confirmation message* for Mr. Osburm, who has been pessimistic throughout the session. Consequently, the therapeutic team's main intent is to lift the father, who has been a bit penalized by today's session.

The *second part* of this intervention contains a classic technique of the strategic approach to family therapy, commonly called "prescription of the homeostasis" (consequently, also of the symptom). What *novelty* is brought to the system by this prescription?

We think that by bringing Benjamin to the session, the other family members were expecting the therapeutic team to openly demand that a change take place, to deplore the fact that the child was still being tardy for school, and to implore the child to behave differently— everything that common sense considers to be right and just. Instead, after a discussion of no more than half an hour, the therapeutic team's conclusions are just the opposite: "Continue just as you are" (taking for granted that this will entail a great effort). This advice is valid for Benjamin (who expected to be told he should go to school like all the other kids), for the mother and father (who expected to be told they should be better parents), and for

David, too (who has the Sword of Damocles hanging over his head, but doesn't have to do anything to avoid it).

This prescription is made acceptable and understandable by means of a simple metaphor that we often use in such cases, the metaphor of the negative.

We presume that these conclusions are unexpected, though we are unable to evaluate if they constitute a *therapeutic novelty* for this particular family system. In order to determine this, we must wait for the long-term retroactions, namely the changes that will, in time, take place.

THIRD SESSION: THE DRAMATIC RETROACTION

PRESESSION

After a long time lapse (more than a month), the family has returned for their third session, once again without the patient. The therapists hypothesize that someone, scared by the intervention, decided not to take him along. We attempt to make a connection with the data available, in order to make the events of the therapeutic process, the behaviors tied to the symptom, and the recent developments in the system somehow correspond. A hypothesis that comes to mind concerning the history of the problem is that when the parents separated there was a very tight alliance between the father and his sons (let us recall that during the presession interview Mr. Osburm had stated that his wife was, at times, treated as an outsider). From the very first session, it had been hypothesized that the symptom's function had been to call the mother back into the family. As a matter of fact, the mother's retroaction to the identified patient's behaviors had been to abandon her night work, which she had refused to do a year before—in other words, before the appearance of the symptoms. The therapeutic team, however, feels that the mother's game had a much wider scope: She hasn't just returned, she has broken the father–Benjamin–David alliance; she has gotten closer to her in-laws, particularly to Mr. Osburm's mother, by choosing to work in their store. The father's retroaction at the sight of the new mother–Benjamin –paternal grandmother (and maybe even grandfather) alliance is, logically enough, depression. We can hypothesize that he is now counting on an alliance with David (the only one left).

With regard to Benjamin's absence, the therapists think that the second session's conduct was too peaceful, that the prescription of homeostasis (by definition, a highly antihomeostatic intervention in itself) has excessively destabilized the system, which has gotten scared, gone beyond the simple prescription, and worsened.

With regard to conduct, today's session will be used to verify the hypothesis *on the function of the symptom for the parents*. Information on the parents' reactions to Benjamin's behaviors will be sought, in addition to their *proposed solutions*, their *differences* of behavior towards their sons, and their *future expectations*. A conduct that follows these criteria cannot but introduce the *subject of the couple* into therapy, it is thus an informative conduct for the family since it *directly establishes the idea that the parents are somehow connected to the problem*.

The information that the mother will give at the end of the session stems from this observation; and it cannot be considered fortuitous since it is crucial for the intervention and for the whole history of the case. It fits the conduct techniques used, and has been actively sought by the therapist through his questions and punctuations.

SESSION

According to the report the parents have made about Benjamin's behaviors—refusal to wash himself, refusal to go to school (or anywhere else), and aggressiveness, especially toward his mother and David—he is most definitely showing signs of psychotic disorder. The parents have openly expressed their inability in dealing with these behaviors. The therapist questions David.

T: OK, listen, David, in our opinion, why are Mom and Dad–maybe your Father more so than your mother–why do they think, they seem convinced, I mean, that Benjamin doesn't pay any attention to what they say?

D: (Visibly embarrassed, he does not answer.)

M: (Interrupts.) Do you think Benjamin listens to us?

D: No, not really. Quite seldom.

T: (Interrupts.) Yes, that's what your parents said . . . both your parents, but in your opinion, how did they get this idea?

D: (He does not answer.)

F: (To David.) Is it just our idea, or is it the truth? I mean, are we the only ones that think so, or is it really like this?

D: (He hurriedly answers.) No, it seems true, it's true.

F: So? David, I think *you should try to feel a little more at ease.* Don't you know what to say?

D: Eh?

M: (To David.) What did you say when he refused to come today? "For Heaven's sake, why didn't you just bring him here to Milan?"

D: Yes.

M: And what did I answer? "Because I wasn't able to convince him." (Her tone is aggressive.)

D: And I told you that you should have let him stay at home.

M: Leaving him home alone is no solution! So, I think he doesn't listen.

D: (Completely confused.) Eh?

After having questioned the family on the course of a usual day and on Mrs. Osburm's new job (in that respect everything is going just fine), the therapist asks how their relatives feel about the problem's worsening. On this topic, the father seems to be filled with discouragement.

T: (Speaking to the father.) OK, but what about the future? What are your ideas? What do you think will happen if the situation continues like this . . .

F: (Interrupts.) Well, I think that in the future there will be an additional problem, that hasn't been brought about by you, but . . .

T: (Interrupts.) We have something to do with this problem? Us?

F: Your hypothesis, about . . . David.

M: (Interrupts.) David . . . that we should worry about David.

F: That we should worry more about David, thus, that's an additional . . . even if, until now, David hasn't had any manifestations . . .

T: (Interrupts.) But what do you mean when you say that you now have an additional problem—worrying about David?

F: Yes, because last time you said: "My impression, the one I had last time, has been confirmed . . ."

T: Of course.

F: That you should have worried more about David.

T: Of course.

F: You also said that the remark was backed by statistics . . .

T: (Interrupts.) On the basis of similar . . .

M: (Interrupts.) Cases.

F: On the basis of similar cases . . .

T: Of course, of course.

F: "You are a high risk family," and so on.

T: Of course.

F: Well, you see, we were conditioned by this, now I'm always worrying about David, I mean . . . sooner or later . . .

T: (Interrupts.) You mean . . . you're saying that you are almost more worried about David than you are for Benjamin.

M: (Interrupts.) Yes, but in a different way.

F: Well, it's hard to make comparisons like this. I can't . . .

T: Well, but we're not asking you to give us a detailed, scientific answer. You mean to tell us that, on top of your worries for Benjamin, we have just added worries about David, too?

F: I hope I shall never have to truly worry about it, I mean I hope, but I don't know . . .

T: You hope, in the sense that you already are worried?
M: (To her husband.) Are you worried about David?
F: Well, actually yes, yes, I am! But I don't know what could happen; how it would manifest itself.

The therapist asks Mr. Osburm how he sees the patient's situation in the future. Mr. Osburm responds by saying that he thinks it will worsen. Mr. Osburm is then questioned on his and his family's reactions if the situation were really to worsen.

F: I think we have two problems, if you will. Benjamin doesn't want to go to school, and this is a fact . . . and also a problem. Secondly, he has outbursts of anger and aggressiveness . . .
T: (Interrupts.) Yes, and this is another problem.
F: This is another problem. Now, if we want to put these two problems together, and say what the future might hold; well, with respect to Benjamin . . . I don't know, I don't think the situation will improve, it will certainly worsen, I don't know. I do know, however, that he won't go to school . . .
T: (Interrupts.) OK, now . . . Let's pretend, as you say, that Benjamin will continue refusing to go to school and that he will become more aggressive. Now, how do you see the situation?
(Pause)
F: The other day, as in the past, we had been talking about the possibility . . . well, of putting him, I don't know, in an institution, a "collegio"[4] or something. . . . It's something we've always said . . . just to . . .
M: (Interrupts.) No, but . . . I'm against a "collegio," I'm sorry.
T: An institution?
M: A "collegio?" shutting him up in a "collegio?"
T: (Overlapping.) A "collegio."
F: (To his wife.) You're against it?
M: Absolutely!

---

[4]In this context, "collegio" means a boarding school that works like an institution, and it is meant as a place where "bad boys" are sent; hence, this choice would be a punishment and an expulsion of the patient.

F: I'm against this idea, too. I have always been against it, and I have always said so.

M: I'm sorry, but things would just get worse if we were to send him away to a "collegio," we certainly wouldn't be helping him by sending him away to school, I'm sorry.

T: Yes, but when . . .

F: (Interrupts.) But at this point how can we help him? I don't know.

T: But, I mean, so what do you think? If the situation worsens . . . I seem to understand, for example . . .

F: (Interrupts.) Let's give some examples, how could he get worse? Because I don't know, worse than it is now . . .

T: (Overlapping.) Let's pretend that Benjamin . . . well, "how could he get worse? . . . I think we're just at the beginning . . .

At this point, the therapist throws a bombshell by compiling a list of the problem's most catastrophic developments. The father reacts symmetrically and the two have a short symmetrical escalation, which results in a loss of neutrality for the therapist. The therapist then proceeds in soliciting information on the *parental couple's differences* with regard to the problem.

T: (Speaking to Mr. Osburm.) Same questions as your wife's, I'm asking you what your wife thinks.

F: I wouldn't know what my wife is thinking.

T: No idea?

F: I just think she is a bit more optimistic than . . .

T: You. That she is more optimistic than you are.

F: Slightly.

T: Yes, slightly.

F: Well, I mean, she has been in the past . . . but now, I don't know . . .

T: Do you agree?

M: Yes, but now . . . I mean, the last few days I've been wondering if it's us . . . I mean William and myself, who don't provide sufficient safety for the child. I mean, in my opinion, Benjamin is afraid. Do you know we had been separated for two years? I don't know if . . .

T: Yes, you got back together a year ago, didn't you?

M: Yes, and I think that the fault was mine; in the past, sometimes when I was really tired, and they would drive me crazy . . .

T: (Interrupts.) When you were separated, I think, the children . . . the children stayed with your husband?

M: Yes, they stayed with their Dad.

T: And you, you were out?

M: Yes, I was out.

T: Then you decided to return, why?

M: Well, I just decided to return . . . (She pauses.)

T: I mean, I don't know, was it because of your husband, the children . . . why did you come back? . . .

M: (Interrupts.) Well, mainly because of the children, and then, also for my husband. But in my opinion . . . I mean . . . well . . . we aren't really . . . close, but . . . maybe the child sees us a bit detached . . . and he doesn't feel safe, and, in the past, sometime, and I blame myself for this, you know, when I was tired, or exasperated, because they gave me a hard time, I would say: "I'm leaving," but I mean, I would just say it, I wouldn't mean it, you know, but clearly the child, well, he suffered.

To confirm her sense of guilt, Mrs. Osburm states that lately she often cries in response to the patient's behaviors. A good solution, for her, would be to remain calm so as to make the child feel safe, but she declares that she can't and defines herself as impulsive, abnormal, and at one point says, "I guess I'm crazy, too." Mr. Osburm supports his wife's self-definition (which is really a self-designation), and narrates an episode in which the only rational and self-controlled person in the whole family turned out to be him.

POSTSESSION

The therapists feel that they *must somehow free the children*, who seem to be strongly controlled (the mother in particular had used the confusion technique in the course of the session; see p. 164). Since the generational boundaries are not well defined, the two levels must be separated at once, so that the parents begin playing their role as parents and their sons return behaving as children. Hence the intervention will be a *splitting*, namely, an intervention consisting in a subdivision of the system so that just a part of it will be present in future sessions.

However, this intervention must be *plausible* and, at the same time, an *alternative* with respect to the family's world view.

Plausible foundations have been constructed during the session by questions about the parents, but most of all by Mrs. Osburm's last few remarks (fear of the separation, the threats, and the sense of guilt). The intervention's diversity, with respect to the punctuations provided by the mother, consists in the fact that while she assumes the guilt for what has happened, the therapist instead, consistent with his neutrality, makes positive connotations about what the parents have been and are doing for their family and for Benjamin's behaviors. The *restructuring* of the problem, which began in the very first session, progresses: The symptom is defined as a "job" that Benjamin (and soon also David) have taken up in order to keep Mom and Dad together. The parents, however, are not to be blamed for this situation: It's an idea that the children somehow, put into their head.

In order for the message tied to the intervention to be neutral, and also to take advantage of its full potential, Benjamin must be present at the conclusion; for this reason, the therapist closes the session by stating that the conclusions will be given in seven days, when all are present. Naturally(!) they all show up in a week's time, including the patient, to hear the conclusions.

RESTRUCTURING AND SPLITTING IN THE THIRD SESSION

T: First of all, we would like to thank Benjamin for having come today but we must also thank him for not coming the last time. Your absence, in fact, permitted us to understand what we had said during the first session, when you were absent, namely that we were worried about David.

This is a *positive connotation* of the disobedience. While it may appear cryptic, *it is justified* by therapeutic motives.

T: We must now tell you that Benjamin and David both are acting *as if they had the idea* that another separation might take place. This explains their behavior; Benjamin in particular, who is the youngest and also the most sensible, a few months ago began working on *a big project to allow his parents to stay together*. David, too, might begin giving his brother a hand.

This is a *restructuring interpretation* based on a content that emerged during the session, hence a plausible one. Benjamin's behaviors are not symptoms; rather they have a positive meaning. The motive that has generated them is not sickness but sensibility: This is another, less direct, positive connotation of the symptom.

T: In cases like this, when children decide to help their parents, they may even reach the point, as experience has taught us, of *sacrificing everything*, to the point of completely refusing their life as children. In other words, not only refusing to go to school, because one might say: "Well, maybe he just doesn't like school," but instead, beginning to shun their friends, their hobbies, their pastimes, in other words, everything.

The intervention's aims are primarily meanings—in other words, an alternative way of viewing the situation is introduced. The parent's sacrifices (they do everything for their children, or so they say) are coupled with the children's sacrifices for their parents (which we know are veritable sacrifices because of the refusal of things and events that are objectively gratifying).

T: However, we have been able to verify that in situations like this the children's "work," if we might call it that, sometimes is not sufficient. Though they may sacrifice themselves and everything else, it just isn't enough. In this case, we might decide *to aid them in their task*, to give them a hand by taking care of the problem and dealing with the parents **ourselves**.

This is another cryptic message: It isn't enough *for what*? The more the therapist insists on this metaphor, the *more real the message becomes*. It is used to introduce the new therapeutic goal for the subsequent sessions.

T: We have, at this time, decided to meet with just you two, Mr. and Mrs. Osburm, in order to understand why Benjamin and David have this idea, namely that in this family another separation might take place. This is their idea, this is also what we perceived and now this is the motive that had us so worried last time.

The therapist now proceeds with the system's splitting, by creating two well-defined, separate subsystems. The therapy's new goal will now become *working on the couple*, though this decision is justified by the children. It is a first step in bringing all their unresolved problems into the open.

T: We thought it was important that Benjamin be here for these conclusions since, after all, they concern him. So we now ask you to go back and live your life as kids, start playing your old games and so on, because we'll take care of Mom and Dad and though we might not be as good as you, we'll do our best to give you a hand.

The therapist purposely emphasizes Benjamin's presence: "The message is for you." At this time, the supervisor calls him on the intercom system to suggest that he emphasize the splitting even more: On an analogical level, the therapist is on the same level as the children, and he metacommunicates on their role-playing as parents. This should produce the correction of the level.

At this point the father appears to want an explanation, but the therapist stops him.

T: No, no explanations, it's important that these things are not discussed. I would have told you but I felt sure that one of you would ask me, so I'm telling you: I would like you to refrain from discussing these things for at least the next 24 hours. After that, you're free to do as you like.

The *prescription of silence* is particularly useful when one feels that the intervention is in danger of being disqualified. It safeguards the intervention's validity for at least the duration of the prescription of silence. In this case, we may be sure that for at least 24 hours the system will be divided into two subsystems. Afterwards, granted that all retroaction may annul this input, it will be very difficult *to erase the experience*.

The intervention we have presented is most complex since it entails the simultaneous use of various techniques. However, it could generally be defined as a *restructuring*, since the premises, meanings, definitions, and expectations that have sustained, and that are currently present in, the Osburm family, are its main goal. The messages tied to the intervention are many, and introduce to the system various novel and unexpected elements: the positive connotation of Benjamin's absence at the previous session; the redefinition of his behaviors as finalized, voluntary, and well-intentioned choices; the summons of only the sane members to the next sessions (it had been said that Benjamin and David both had "strange ideas"), and so forth.

These messages are linked to the precise techniques chosen from the wide repertory of "techniques of paradoxical intervention."

EVALUATION IN
Chapter 5 | **FAMILY THERAPY**

When illustrating our model we have pointed out how the choice of a particular epistemology is related to precise practical needs and decisions. In particular, our often-declared interest for a scientific approach to clinical work requires the adoption of a definite position with respect to the problem of verification of therapeutic activity. If family therapy is to be a rational and rationalized activity, aimed at the solution of clearly formulated problems through precise techniques applied with rigor, one cannot avoid submitting this activity to evaluation, to a critique that coherently connects premises, actions, and outcomes. Every scientific activity proceeds by validation or refutation of the underlying hypotheses. This must be true also for therapy. Bloch, in his foreword to Hoffman's book, writes that "family therapy is a clinical science. The proof of the validity of its theories is that they generate (or

175

rationalize) actions leading to change in a direction taken to be desirable (by someone who will pay the bill)" (Hoffman 1981). Clinical application is the indirect confirmation of theory.

Having made these premises, we wish to state immediately that reality is far from these programmatic indications: In reality it has been difficult, and still is, to solve the evaluation problem. In our everyday practice we have discovered that it is an arduous enough task trying to establish some sort of guideline that at least makes it possible to gather some information.

A source of complication derives from the fact that, in our field, one cannot speak of evaluation *tout court*: The work of our therapeutic team itself implies a multiplicity of levels of information, different references, and horizontal and vertical relations with the institutions. Each of these levels involves, or should involve, its own verification of the choice undertaken.

We will consider the three aspects that, at this point, concern us the most:

1. An "idiographic" approach to therapy. Every case has its own history, its own hypotheses, and its own personal conclusion. From this point of view, the evaluation must take into consideration, one by one, every single step taken by the therapeutic team in dealing with the problem presented. In particular, this approach concerns the rules of conclusion: When can one say the case is happily concluded?

2. A more general evaluation, implying a judgment of the team's activity and, ultimately, of its therapeutic ability. First and foremost, a generalization requires a choice between the variables and the instruments to be used in relation to the aims and the context of evaluation.

3. An answer to the question "Does family therapy

fulfill the aims of the service?" This should never fail to be addressed in a public-service context, and thus in a center like ours. The answer is not an easy one. It requires a thorough analysis of the institutional context in which one operates as well as of the implicit and explicit requests it demands.

In the next few paragraphs we will consider these three aspects of therapeutic evaluation one by one. With the possible exception of the first, which is more qualitative and consequential to therapy, each will be critically examined. Despite our attempts to give some answers, the reader will mostly encounter questions.

"THE CASE IS CLOSED": VERIFICATION OF THE THERAPEUTIC HYPOTHESIS

RESPONSES TO THE INTERVENTION

As we have already seen in the preceding chapter, therapeutic hypotheses are subject to verification through the intervention. This first verification is not formalized, being tied to a particular moment, to the direct observation of what is happening, and to all the verbal and analogical messages that precede, accompany, and follow the intervention.

Each intervention, in fact, is a communicatory act and therefore implies a proposal of a relationship to the members of the family system on the part of the therapist. The interlocutor (in this case every member) cannot but retroact, thus somehow qualifying the relational message.

The hypotheses we adopt is that every family event that

follows the intervention is to be considered as a response to it. In other words, every subsequent communication somehow qualifies the intervention. Naturally numerous other factors of a nontherapeutic nature, which the therapist does not even suspect the existence of, are involved; consequently this hypothesis is merely an arbitrary punctuation, which defines the therapeutic activity as a stimulus for the system and therapy time as the only influence in its history.

From a temporal point of view we can identify a rough subdivision of the family reactions into two stages: immediate feedback and long-term retroactions.

IMMEDIATE FEEDBACK

The fact that the family cannot but qualify the therapist's message implies that each member of the system will react in accordance with his or her own vision of the intervention's significance and role in the family game. The system's reaction is not always unanimous; on the contrary, since the intervention is restabilizing, almost inevitably someone will feel relieved (from responsibility, designation, or guilt) and someone else will feel the target of the punctuation introduced by the therapists (for example, the internal referring person, when the therapist states that therapy will not take place; or an intrusive member, when the therapist limits his field of influence by a prescription).

According to communication theory, the possible answers to a proposal of relationship are confirmation, rejection, and disconfirmation. What does this mean for the therapist?

Confirmation. The definition of the relationship introduced by the therapist is accepted, both on a verbal and an analogical plane. The interlocutor's position is complementary (consistent with the context).

Rejection. With similar coherence, the therapist's proposal is rejected. It is an implicit recognition of the therapist's right to communicate, but also of one's own right to react symmetrically; therefore it may be defined as a sane reaction.

Disconfirmation. This is not so much a way to react as a whole set of reactions different in intensity and effects—all sharing the same confusion, lack of a clear definition, negation (of the transmitter, of the channel, or of the receiver), and thus a destructive power with respect to the intervention. Typically, answers take the shape of disqualification: elusive answers, literal interpretations of the metaphors (or even metaphorical interpretation of literal messages), status disqualifications ("You are not a therapist"), shifting, redundant or strange questions, and so on.

On an analogical plane, which are the most frequent behaviors transmitting this type of message? In this respect, the family members' facial expressions are enlightening. Typical reactions are:

Evident relief.

Negative-disappointed reaction.

Incoherence–confusion.

Impassiveness.

Each of these reactions can occur according to the goals and behaviors the intervention intended to aim at. They are single reactions, since on a semantic level it is the family members who decipher and understand messages.

Usually the therapist prefers avoiding any disqualification, even the suspect ones (such as symmetrical moves). For this reason he immediately takes leave from the family. Nevertheless, a system's response, however disqualifying or symmetric it may be, is always useful to get a first idea of the impact that the prescription might have on the family game.

The fact that, for example, only after a well-contrived intervention someone recalls something very important (possibly data or circumstances the therapists were unable to bring to light during the interview) is a first validation of the hypotheses. So are the family's questions that tend to bring the patient back in the spotlight after a problem-shifting intervention.

It is important that the therapist answer these last-minute questions consistent with the hypothesis and its definition of the relationship: Since the situation is open to confusion and disqualification, an endeavor must be made in order to elude them, under penalty of jeopardizing the success of the intervention even before the system has been able to elaborate it. Usually every new problem or discussion is put off until the following session—"This could be the topic for future discussion." Sometimes, when asked how they should behave, the paradoxical answer "act spontaneously" is given. These problems can be elegantly prevented by prescribing silence. This may be achieved by saying "it is very important that all we have told you will not be in any way discussed for the next 24 hours." In this way a lot of important information is lost, although the impact of the subsequent message increases. All things considered, an expert therapist can afford the risk of surprises and of possible booby traps of an immediate answer.

In summary, on what basis do the therapists affirm that an intervention has hit the mark? They are quantitative, behavioral-analogical indicators. If the member of the system that the therapists wish to help (cheer up) shows satisfaction; if the identified patient appears visibly relieved after the intervention; if the spokesperson of the family seems disoriented; then there is a good possibility of encountering, at the subsequent session, a changed system.

LONG-TERM RETROACTIONS

The only information that can uphold or dismiss the team's hypothesis is change. It is only the effectiveness of the therapy that, in the absence of set criteria of truth, can support one theory over another.

In between sessions the system readjusts on the basis of the perturbation introduced by the therapeutic activity (both the session and the intervention). The readjustment can be more or less adaptive, or rather it can increase or decrease the autonomy or the future flexibility of the system. In this respect, we are convinced of the importance of a long time lapse between the sessions; the information introduced by the therapeutic process then remains, interacts, and creates new connections. Change brings about change. We just have to give the system some time: There will be a largely unforeseeable readjustment, at times beyond all expectations, surprising even for the therapist.

The changes that have occurred (one can *say* that a change takes place anyway) can or cannot be recognized by the members of the system, and if they are recognized they can be linked, though not necessarily so, to therapy.

A clue to what has taken place in the course of the month or more can be the *familial climate* and the behavior of each member upon the family's return. A more preoccupied or, on the contrary, a more peaceful climate may be installed with respect to the last meeting (quite independent of the system's "reality").

There are some *typical reactions to the disappearance of the symptoms.* The system can relate the message that the problem nonetheless remains (referring to the "negative characteristics" that still remain in the identified patient's personality); or it can deny the disappearance of the dysfunctional behaviors; or it can accurately avoid talking about this during the whole session by side-stepping all of the therapist's questions to focus on other problems (which may become from then on the true focus of therapy).

In order to formulate precise hypotheses on the impact of the intervention, it is necessary to investigate *other behaviors,* too, and precisely those that according to the hypothesis were *tied to the problem* and kept the problem in an unsolved state. The criterion of the disappearing symptom is linked to a change in the family pattern.

Finally, it is important to verify, as far as possible, the *change of interpretation* that has taken place in the premises. This change alone in fact guarantees the system's future ability in dealing with new difficulties without resorting to the symptom.

In summary, the team's attitude with regard to the contents brought by the family is to consider all that has happened as a countermove to the intervention. It is a dangerous, causal attitude, but mitigated by the fact that the therapists are aware that this is only an arbitrary way of viewing things. One could rightly say that the system has changed not thanks to the intervention but in spite of it.

What if the system does not seem to accept the challenge that the intervention implies? Then the tactics chosen must be reconsidered; every effort must be made to discover what did not work in the session; one's own hypotheses on the problem, on the pattern that sustains it, on the system or subsystem involved in its upkeeping, must be reviewed; and if necessary, the problem must be redefined, other "patterns which connect" must be found, and possibly the target system must be enlarged or narrowed.

THE CONCLUSION OF THERAPY

THERAPEUTIC PLAN

The interventions and the sessions follow each other more or less effectively, creating by and by a veritable process, in which the family system and the therapeutic team retroact one with the other and change. The team calls this process a "therapeutic plan." The name seems misleading, suggesting the existence of a predetermined strategy, envisaging the image of a series of steps or stages toward health. Nothing could be more untrue: The concept of a therapeutic process as something linear, which proceeds in an orderly manner toward a goal, is totally inadequate for describing the leaps, turning points, symptomatic explosions, and sudden (and unexplainable) remissions that follow each other in the course of treatment. Furthermore, in this case it is the very concept of predetermination that is put on trial. In fact, if at times the system confirms the therapist's illusion of having foreseen everything just as it happened, there are events (for better or for worse) that take it entirely by surprise. (Systems, after all, are very good at surprising; it is the therapists who most of the time show very little spirit and get angry!)

At a certain moment in the therapy—it can happen after the ten sessions agreed upon, or even after the first consultation—the team feels that it is heading toward closure. We shall not try to specify what we mean by "feel," since this is a very unscientific term.

CRITERIA FOR CONCLUDING

We can examine, first of all, the *system's message.* If in a coherent manner the family members, or their official speaker (in every system there is an individual who carries out this task), communicates that an equilibrium has been reached, that the problem has been cleared up, or that the system does not feel the need to continue therapy, it appears obvious that another session is impossible (the therapeutic context definition would be lacking and there would not be any contents to speak of).

A second indicator comes to us from the relationship, in particular from the *incongruencies* between analogical and verbal messages. It often happens that a system continues to attend the sessions (thus implicitly confirming its engagement) while, on a content plane, it communicates that everything is much better. In this case, it is necessary to establish whether the system has come just to be polite, since it had an appointment; in which case the family would never dream of dropping out unless the therapist explicitly prescribes it. However, it might also be possible that the verbal message "everything is ok." is really just a disguise of the problem that the system indirectly recognizes and denies. Hence, it becomes necessary to make these problems surface through the conduct techniques already described.

An obvious indicator of the state of things is the

presence or absence of a symptom. It is a double-edged weapon since the therapist never knows at what point the symptomatic behavior really is; at the most, he might have a few indications of the magnitude of the problem if it is manifested during the session, or in the case of objective symptoms like the eating habits of anorexic patients. We usually assume that all the therapist's ideas are tied to what is said and done during the session, hence one does not work on the symptom but rather on the ideas connected with it and on the information given by the system's members.

For this reason we have placed the system's messages at the top of the list: Saying that the problem has disappeared is in itself a demand for dismissal, or a message of disengagement apart from the truth of its content.

The last change indicator is the style of the familial communication during the session, which may give information on what has been learned through the restructured family patterns, the clarity of the communications, and the intra- and intersystemic relationships. It is most important to compare the first and last sessions (this is made possible thanks to the videotape of the session) since this gives a very clear picture of the changes that are occurring.

HOW A CONCLUSION IS REACHED

Even in the case of a conclusion, it is hard to give a set formula. This is an extremely idiosyncratic moment, in the sense that it is dependent on the history of the therapy, on the context, on the therapist's preferences, in addition to a long series of causal factors. At this time the therapist must not forget his model and the premises and take advantage of this last occasion to make an input that will increase the system's ability for self-recovery. At times, the closure becomes a privileged time in the intervention; we affirm this in order to remove any thoughts that the decision to end the therapy coincides with the recovery and the solution to all the problems, but also that this decision is not up to the therapist. Actually, the case in which the team decides to simply close and dismiss the family is not the only possible solution, and it most likely is not the more widely used in our setting.

Let us consider the various possibilities in the next three sections.

The Family Unilaterally Puts an End to Therapy. In the event that the family puts an end to therapy, the possibilities are that:

The problem persists.

The problem does not persist, but a real restructuring has not occurred ("escape to health").

A restructuring has taken place (with or without gratitude toward the therapists).

The Therapist Unilaterally Puts an End to Therapy. In this case there may be:

A stalemate. Ending therapy takes advantage of the restructuring power and of the novelty of the closure with respect to the system's expectations (for example, admission of impotence or end of contract).

A false closure. Here, for example, the therapist might say that therapy is dangerous, we shall meet only for a consultation or consolation session; or therapy may stay open albeit with a long time lapse between the sessions.

Closure with an often paradoxical comment reenforcing or amplifying change.

"Agreed" Closure. The therapist suggests or prescribes to the family to spontaneously decide if it no longer needs therapy. For example, the family may be asked to call back if it decides to continue the therapy, or in the case of the appearance of new problems. The premise, however, is that the family will not show up again; in the case that it does, the demand for therapy brings about a clear definition of the relationship as therapeutic, and thus it opens the possibility of concluding in a few sessions, this time for good.

From the above cases, we can conclude that the closing pattern is the following: One of the two systems involved in the therapeutic relationship goes "meta" with respect to the coupling established in time between the two and opts for a new rule: to get out of the game. The other may or may not accept it (usually the other system is in such a position that it must accept, but not without a redefinition).

From the therapists' point of view (but only from their point of view!), the "induced" closure, being under their supervision, can be positively evaluated; the noninduced but sane one (since it can be explained with the available tools) is just as positive (this in itself is hard to accept), but the true dropout—the unexpected, unexplainable, and thus insane one—is frustrating and consequently creates new needs, especially that of knowing what happened.

IS FAMILY THERAPY SUCCESSFUL?
A CLINICAL EVALUATION

Let us now deal with a more generalized problem from those presented in the preceding subchapters. In order to evaluate the effectiveness of one's actions in a single case, it is sufficient to make a hypothesis. If we hypothesize that the family pattern is structured around the problem in a certain way; if we hypothesize that in order to have an impact on it one must enter the game in a certain way at a certain point; if we hypothesize that what happens afterward is a positive change; then we can hypothesize that we have done a good job.

Hence with this method one can come up with many case reports, descriptions of isolated cases, that are interesting and full of information. However, when a therapist has chosen a career in therapy and embraced a model of intervention, and when this model follows the scientific method, then these qualitative and subjective evaluations are no longer valid. One looks for objectivity and comparability of data, generalization, and as far as possible (since we are dealing with clinical science) repeatability. We have thus reached the central issue of this chapter, clinical evaluation.

A clinical evaluation is a standardized and systemic collection of data by means of which one can draw sufficiently rigorous conclusions both on single cases (follow-up) and on comparisons between several different therapies (catamnestic research).

The tool for clinical evaluation is *catamnesis*, namely a reexamination of the case after a predetermined and equal interval, whose aim is gaining information on the changes that took place after therapy and on the problems that still exist. In other words, we have to determine if the changes are long lasting and how they have influenced the system's life and capacity for adaptation.

What is evaluated during catamnesis? Certainly not everything: the territory is not comprehensible either through a relatively long interaction like the one that occurs in the session or through the brief contact of a catamnestic interview.

The first step toward rationalizing catamnesis consists in establishing which items of information are, according to our hypothesis, crucial for the purpose of drawing a map of the situation. These items of information will be the same as those used for tracing the system's map before and after therapy—that is, information on "differences" and "relationship." In this case, however, the situation is entirely different: The therapists' goal is neither the construction of new hypotheses nor intervention. Now the therapists are simply observers, not therapists. Their task is to make a comparison between the final hypothesis (easily drawn from the transcripts) and the actual situation of the family and its members.

Obtaining the information desired from one of them should be easy because they ought to know, more than us, what we need to know, and also because it is assumed that they have learned the rules of systemic communication or differences. However, this learning should not be taken for granted, since it constitutes the outcome of the therapeutic process we have to evaluate. A member of the system might very well lie during catamnesis and the therapist would never know; or a family member could deny everything or use other tricks, disqualify therapy, or only partially answer the questions.

The only data obtainable with a certain degree of certainty is the request for further therapy (if the family requests it).

CRITERIA FOR CLINICAL EVALUATION

In view of the observations made above, it becomes imperative to define the criteria for structuring an informative catamnestic situation, in other words a situation in which one can accept the data gathered with a certain degree of confidence. In our opinion, this should ensure that catamnesis becomes a routine activity and becomes a primary goal.

To rationalize means to examine the various stages of a research activity (de facto, catamnesis is one of them), to define them, and to endeavor to understand how they may be carried out in accordance with the model. Research methodology cannot prescind from premises. The principal stages of research activity are:

Definition of goals.

Choice of the object of study and the aspects to be considered.

Choice of the most suitable methods and tools.

We will discuss each stage in turn.

DEFINITION OF GOALS

We may consider both the context characterized by a routine gathering of information at given intervals, the one more widely used and familiar to us; and more specific contexts (studies on particular samples, such as dropouts, on those systems that have undergone a given process, or on those families sent to the center with specific purposes by another public service agency). Obviously, hypotheses will differ in each case, thus requiring specific inquiries and questions that hardly agree with the systematic and standardized approach implied by an information-gathering activity.

A possible solution could be to have the family undergo a follow-up in any case, as is now already being done, and to ask more targeted questions only in particular instances and in view of specific purposes, naturally explaining the reasoning behind this choice. Such a solution, however, would call for complete research facilities, for both the singling out and evaluating the questions and the answers.

THE OBJECT OF STUDY AND THE ASPECTS TO BE CONSIDERED

If the purpose of catamnesis is to evaluate the effectiveness of family therapy we must, first of all, define what we mean by "family therapy" and "effectiveness."

It should be clear that therapy may be considered from different angles and differently defined. Each definition entails a different objective for our research.

One definition could be the following: Family therapy is a process in which two systems, the family and our team, interact until the former (for different reasons) thinks it no longer needs help. In this case, the request for therapy becomes the privileged object of evaluation: If the family no longer needs therapy, then the criterion has been met.

In a traditional perspective, therapy may be regarded as an activity aimed at the symptomatic member's recovery. The crucial question thus becomes whether or not the symptoms have disappeared or, less simplistically, does the identified patient lead a satisfying and normal life, with respect to his or her age and social and cultural stereotypes?

Alternatively, if we wish to include, in accordance with the systemic model, all the family members in the problem, we might ask ourselves are the family patterns "saner"? Has the problem shifted into other areas or parts of the system? The literature often focuses on this point and suggests an analysis of such aspects as clarity in family communications, interpersonal confirmation, level conflicts, differentiations, and so on, depending on the theory that inspires it.

As we have already stated, a change in the system's erroneous premises may become the "metagoal" of therapy. In order to verify whether this goal has been achieved one must take into consideration the family members' interpretation of their own past, present, and future situation.

Each of the aspects listed above is by itself an enormous simplification of that complex and multifaceted event that is change. Only a comprehensive look at all of these criteria can do justice to an event that is irreducible. For this reason, our catamnesis tries to answer all the questions we have formulated in these few pages.

Is this information, however, sufficient to confirm our choices? The indicators (end of the request for therapy, disappearance of the symptoms, restructuring of patterns and ideas) give us an idea of the effectiveness of therapy but, once again, it all remains within the realm of hypotheses, as it should. From our point of view, the effectiveness of our intervention is beyond a simple and direct definition, both on a practical and theoretical plane.

THE MOST SUITABLE METHODS AND TOOLS

The method to be adopted in gathering the catamnestic data must be contingent with the model. This implies that oversimplification is not allowed. The literature on clinical evaluation is packed with surveys that have adopted "objective" methods: scales, questionnaires, quantified measures that make averaging out possible, the probability estimate and the evaluation of the data's significance. What the authors aim at is generalization, comparison, and above all, objectivity.

However, though conceptual and methodological rigor is among our values, objectivity is not. On the contrary, at the beginning of this book we admitted a position decisively in favor of a model and a working hypothesis that goes against illusions of objectivity. Consequently, we hope that the method will hold complexity in the highest respect just like the whole of our work.

RETURN TO COMPLEXITY

One of the weaknesses of the so-called objective methods and tools is the underlying idea that whomever the observer and whatever his or her goals and the context in which data are gathered, facts remain facts.

However, we who ascribe a great significance to the therapist's hypothesis and think, like Bateson, that ends should not be separated from means (Bateson 1972) and that context is the privileged "matrix of meaning"; we who are convinced that ideas can influence events, cannot speak of verification in a traditional sense.

If one wishes to take into full account the complexity of a situation such as therapy, which is above all an interactive process, one must attribute to the participants in the process and to the parameters involved their due weight.

This implies first accepting the observer's role in the information-gathering process. In an approach like ours, rather than a "variable of disturbance" the observer becomes the measuring meter par excellence. For this reason, catamnesis is based on a method parallel to that of therapeutic conduct and following the same guidelines:

> Clarity in the definition of the context (as nontherapeutic: Every contact with the system carries with it the danger of a new engagement).

> Neutral, circular, and professional attitude (it must be emphasized that therapists are not out to judge anyone, nor to seek acclaim and gratification).

Clear and precise hypotheses (information is not just "out there"; we must construct it).

Questions as useful and targeted as possible. What is being asked and how it is being asked has an enormous influence on the interlocutor's expectations and contributes to defining the context.

CATAMNESIS: SOME PROBLEMS

Although we have already dealt with the conceptual and practical problems we encounter in establishing the rules of catamnestic conduct, we cannot say we have thoroughly solved them. The first problem concerns the setting or situation: One wonders if an interview is the ideal technique for a follow-up. In view of several considerations we have set it aside, at least for now.

One reason is that an interview, an involving situation per se, recalls the setting in which therapy takes place. Not only does it involve the problem of finding a good definition for the context as something different from therapeutic sessions, but it might also cause the risk of inducing a new engagement, and it raises the question of how to define the context as something else with respect to the other therapeutic sessions.

Another related problem is who will hold the catamnestic interview? The therapist should be excluded (although his presence might be useful, if not as supervisor, at least in formulating the catamnestic hypotheses). Besides, this would increase the cost of the service, as well as require additional facilities (such as larger office spaces), increased personnel, and so on.

On the other hand, only an interview with the whole system allows a direct, live observation of the interaction. This advantage, however, raises another problem: Certain therapies end with a separation (of the son from his parents, of the marital couple, of the family system from the rest of their relatives) or with a splitting (after a few interviews with all the cohabitants, therapy proceeds with a subsystem only). In these cases, who will be included in the system to be summoned for a checkup? And what implicit or explicit messages will this convocation imply? Not to mention the "objective" problems in answering the convocation; for example, a great number of our families travel from other regions to attend therapy; would they do the same for catamnesis?

Once the interview had been discarded (though it still remains a privileged tool of observation), the problem was finding a situation sufficiently standardized to be recorded on the information card.

Thus our catamneses are conducted on the phone. The operator calls the number that has been left to us by the family and speaks with one of the session's participants, explaining the reasons for calling and asking a fixed set of questions:

Do the problems that led you to seek help at the Family Therapy Center still exist?

How are things now, in relation to the problems that led you to seek help at the Family Therapy Center?

Since then, have you gone to other therapists for help with these problems? If yes, whom did you go to?

Have any other problems arisen? Which ones?

The therapist then reexamines the information card and draws a conclusion.

This is the procedure currently used, but we are not unaware of its shortcomings. The first criticism concerns the relation between catamnestic hypothesis (when we do have one) and data, as well as between data and final hypothesis, which we feel is too mediated. Even teamwork, which should be a main characteristic, is left to chance and performed only occasionally with no fixed time or place.

An additional remark is worth mentioning: For reasons often beyond our control, our staff is not able to fully take advantage of the opportunities offered by the setting. The context we work in, in fact, should put us in a privileged position. It allows a direct comparison of the system before and after therapy: The family's entire change process is always available for reexamination, reconsideration, and reinterpretation, thanks to the video recording of all the sessions and to the punctual (at least, it should be so) gathering of data into reports. If properly used, these tools would allow for the formulation of precise catamnestic hypotheses taking into account all that has happened during therapy. Even after several months from the conclusion of treatment, therapists have access to all the information they might need.

Instead, what regularly happens is that once confronted by catamnesis, after one year from the end of therapy, one goes crazy. We do not mean that catamnesis is a dramatic aspect of a case. On the contrary, sometimes it is the most gratifying one, since it gives the therapist the joy of discovering that everything is going well; that the identified patient is now studying, working, married, or traveling around the world; that the problematic child is now calm; that the couple "works." Although most often merit goes "to the Virgin Mary," "to Auntie," or "to the newborn grandson," in reality it is family therapy that works.

What is tragic for us as "complex" family therapists is

not being able to fully understand what has happened, to explain those cases that do not seem completely resolved, and to make valid generalizations, and also realizing that not all the relevant information has been used. In other words, what is still lacking is a rigorous and satisfactory tool, and one consistent with the model.

IS FAMILY THERAPY THE OPTIMAL TREATMENT? EVALUATION OF FAMILY THERAPY IN AN INSTITUTIONAL CONTEXT

After dealing with case report and catamnestic research as two levels of evaluation of our work, we now pass to the "meta" level and to another issue: Does our kind of family therapy fulfill not only a criterion of therapeutic effectiveness but also the patients' initial demands? Or, as Hoffman puts it, is "he who pays the bill" happy with our work?

The problem has at least two interrelated aspects: (1) the cost-effectiveness ratio and (2) the relation between systemic premises and the goals of the center.

THE COST-EFFECTIVENESS RATIO

Family therapy is costly. In terms of material resources, since it requires a team of trained professionals, longer work hours than other forms of therapy, additional personnel, a special setting (one-way mirrors, microphones, video recorders, therapy rooms, supervision rooms, meeting rooms, and so on). In terms of psychological resources, since it is new and implies increased organizational effort, a willingness to change, and flexibility.

The need for establishing the cost-effectiveness ratio is peculiar to public services. A private therapist's primary goal is to satisfy the client, and if he or she does have outside liaisons, they are mostly "cultural" rather than concrete. Our client, instead, is the center, and ultimately society itself.

Nonetheless, we have no ready-made answers, or rather we would be able to answer only if a number of oversimplifications could be made. We could divide, for example, the population that has come into contact with the center into three groups: resolved cases, unresolved cases, and untreated cases (if there are any).

Provided that this were possible, what purpose would it serve? Besides, it would be easy for us (as for all clinicians) to insert the majority of the cases into the first group, since ultimately we are the ones who decide which cases are resolved or not.

After all, what is a failed case? Dropouts themselves (a therapist's biggest fear) may be sane and a symptom, as we all know, may be positively redefined in thousands of ways. Not to mention the problem of comparing these discrete observations with costs or, worse still, with other observations just as discrete and arbitrary concerning other services and forms of therapy.

THE RELATION BETWEEN SYSTEMIC PREMISES AND THE AIMS OF THE CENTER

If we move on to the ideological dimension, the comparison becomes even more problematic. In the first place, as for the outside world, there is not always an open attitude, which considers every model arbitrary. Furthermore, the model we have adopted is, on a conceptual plane, particularly difficult and provocative, since it does not follow the more traditional and socially accepted attitude toward mental disorders. It cannot abstain, at any rate, from coming to terms with the other models since it has to cohabit with them: Hospitals exchange patients and have common communication channels (inefficient though they may be); a few families come to us with a therapy already in progress (individual psychotherapy, pharamacological therapy, and so on).

Which is the "right" model? Evidently, all and none. This question must be asked, however, on a different plane, for the context on which we operate cannot be, in any case, forgotten. That is what we stress the most in training young therapists and operators. Context analysis is important, being a prerequisite of clinical work, and the range of possible contexts infinite, almost as many as our students.

For our part, we endeavor to optimize our relations with sister institutions so as to coordinate goals and methods. If a family is incorrectly sent to us our work will be undermined.

Besides, this should be a vital phase for whoever applies a systemic approach. Each working environment demands modifications in the model, which can be rarely used in the same exact way as we have adopted and described in the preceding pages.

The Centro per lo Studio e la Terapia della Famiglia, as we have already noted several times, is a privileged case, more than rare, being not only a center where family therapy is implemented (and researched) in a public service context (an exceptional case in itself), but also one whose objective is family therapy alone. This context cannot be reproduced within all the other (sociopsycho-pedagogic, psychosocial, and so on) public health services and institutions which have a variety of aims and references and whose problems are alien to us.

In summary, we are able to affirm that family therapies

work, but only within a peculiar model, democratic both in the definition of its values and positive, acceptable behaviors, and in the "metaevaluation" of other approaches to psychotherapy.

How do institutions (public health service, administrators and politicians, the police department) feel about it?

How do the agencies (such as medical advisory centers) with which we are in contact and that send their families to us feel about it?

How does the uncle, friend, or therapist feel about it?

Understandably enough, this chapter ends with several questions that, like many others we raised, remain unanswered. Probably, the answer to many of them is not even up to us. Working with a paradigm "based on complexity" is a hard enough task: Complexity and circularity undermine a scientist's and a clinician's self-confidence. Always keeping in mind the many levels of our interventions and giving up the quick and easy simplifications and instructions of the more traditional scientific methodologies requires a great effort to avoid nihilism. Our decision to favor complexity is not, and should not be, an alibi.

On the contrary, we regard the awareness of the intrinsic, extreme complexity of living systems, of human relations, and of every activity such as ours as a constructive choice that we feel could serve as a guideline for action, possibly in new directions. It is a challenge (never fully answered) to seek rigor, to constantly question our hypotheses, to take on the role of instigator, and to refute every scientific or clinical stereotype.

CLINICAL CASE: EPILOGUE

In this section we will present the final three sessions, and discuss our conclusions, for the case study that has continued through the preceding three chapters.

FOURTH SESSION: THE IMPORTANCE OF TIME IN THE THERAPEUTIC PROCESS

PRESESSION

After a reexamination of the previous session's transcripts, the therapist noticed they had made a mistake in summoning the Osburms (for their fourth session) after just three weeks from the restructuring intervention. In our work, *the time factor is of utmost importance*: Following an intervention, the family must be given ample time to elaborate the information and to find a new equilibrium, especially if the intervention, as in this case, entails a very large restructuring. The presession hypothesis was thus just a tool to see which significant retroactions, with respect to the symptomatic behavior, they might expect and, following such a hypothesis, it was decided that under no circumstances would they work on the problem, and they would especially steer clear of talking about the children. Instead, the whole session revolved around the need to "understand why Benjamin and David thought that their parents would once again separate," and thus on the reconstruction of the couple's history. This choice of conduct was functional to the emphasis that had been placed on the splitting during the session: The interest kept moving away from the patient and onto the parents.

SESSION

William and Joan got married after David's birth. After a few years, William had an affair and told his wife who, initially, adapted to the situation. When he ended the relationship ("it wasn't good for the children"), Joan asked him for a separation and left the children with him. For a few years, William took care of the children while his wife occasionally came to see them. As the years passed, however, Joan began spending all her free time with her sons (in the meantime, she had left the man she had been living with and had started working nights). Finally, when her father died, on William's suggestion she went with her mother to live with William and the children. They all lived together for six months, until her mother, having recovered from her husband's death, went back to her house while Joan decided to stay.

When the therapist asks them "Would you have gotten back together if you hadn't had the children?" he answers "Probaby yes"; she instead answers "Probably not."

Their whole history is a series of *repeated disconfirmations*: He affirms he was against the separation, but he consented; he says that his children came before everything else (he left his lover for them), but nonetheless he does everything in his power to shut his wife out, although he admits the children suffer because of it; she left him for another man, but then she "realized her place was with her children"; he didn't want her back "because by that time I was used to living in a threesome system," but then he calls her back, together with his mother-in-law; he continues to say that he does everything for his children while, in fact, he takes care of them as little as possible.

HYPOTHESIS

During the fourth session, a few hypotheses that hadn't yet been confirmed in the previous sessions were, at last, confirmed. Disconfirmations seem to be the mainstay of family communications: This justifies not only Benjamin's sufferings but everyone else's, too. The parental couple seems to need the alibi of their children in order to stay together, and also to leave; this allows them to avoid metacommunicating about their relationship. The children are constantly used as the pretext for their parents' decisions, and this makes them feel unloved and worthless (the father hardly takes care of them and their mother left them when she wanted to). Benjamin's symptomatic behavior may only have originated as a result of *a long history of such disconfirmations*.

However, according to the parents, changes are currently taking place, such as an increased definition of the relationships between themselves as a couple, and also among other family members.

It must be noted that throughout the session, Mr. and Mrs. Osburm were able to speak of themselves without ever referring to the problem and the children; an item of information that emerged almost by chance is that as of two months ago Joan and William have resumed sleeping together. (They had "forgotten" to mention that they were sleeping in separate rooms . . . since Benjamin was really the problem!)

Due to the incompleteness of the retroactions to the splitting intervention, the therapists decided that the emphasis provided by the session centered on the couple was sufficient; at this time, an intervention which would quickly reunite the couple might be dangerous and result in a fresh outbreak of the symptoms or in the appearance of new problems in order to stop the definition of the relationship. In such cases a *reassuring intervention* with respect to the change is sometimes conducted. But in this instance this was not possible, since by choice no hypotheses had been made with regard to Benjamin's situation and thus the therapeutic team had no information available (no information had been solicitated from the parents, nor did they volunteer any). Hence, the session was simply closed and another appointment was fixed in two months.

FIFTH SESSION: THE THERAPEUTIC TEAM'S GRATIFICATION

PRESESSION

By the fifth session, the therapists had been expecting great retroactions: According to the hypotheses, the symptom no longer had meaning and consequently no reason to exist. Thus, when choosing a conduct technique, once again, it was decided to privilege the couple because only a definition of the couple's relationship (both in the case that they would really get back together, or that they would permanently part) could make Benjamin's behavior useless.

With regard to contents, it was decided that they should investigate Joan and William's future plans, in order to understand how they perceived their future as a couple. Once again, it was decided that talk of the children should be kept to a minimum, just a few remarks in order to gain information on Benjamin's situation with respect to the symptoms. For this reason, the therapist decided that each time the conversation would shift over to the children, he would emphasize that the session's aim was "to clear up the couple's precarious situation" for the children's sake.

SESSION

Information about Benjamin is provided immediately. William states that after the fourth session, the child has begun to attend school regularly and that the other problematic behaviors have also disappeared. The couple's evaluation of the changes that have taken place differs. Mr. Osburm thinks there have been improvements, but he is nonetheless still a little worried. For Mrs. Osburm (and David too, or so they say), the problem has been completely resolved. The whole session centers around the restructuring intervention—namely, why, though they present themselves as a couple becoming more and more close and getting along well, the children still seem to think the contrary and behave as if a separation were imminent.

HYPOTHESIS

The splitting has worked: The parents come to therapy together, they speak of their relationship, they have been sleeping in the same bed now for three months, they are even, to a certain extent, able to foresee a future together. . . . Most of all, the intervention has succeeded in freeing the i.p. from the game. Benjamin has resumed his life normally and it is quite unlikely that the symptoms will ever return, if his mother and father are kept busy planning their future life together.

The only real danger is that someone might make a "homeostatic move." For example, Mr. Osburm, who is still a little puzzled and keeps blaming his wife, might get David involved now that Benjamin is out of the picture. This might happen because the couple's problems have not disappeared nor have they been completely cleared up: Double, reciprocated messages, especially on their staying together, still remain; they each seem to be afraid of revealing their true feelings to their partner.

Hence these observations make clear the need for an intervention that recognizes the changes that have taken place without emphasizing them, that accepts Mr. Osburm's perplexities concerning the real motives behind the change. Once again, the intervention is centered around the couple: Their situation has not changed; consequently, one doesn't understand how a change can have taken place. Refusing to accept the fact that they had really changed should have strengthened, according to the therapist's hypotheses, their union and automatically improved Benjamin's problem.

INTERVENTION

T: We have evaluated the data you have provided us today, and frankly we must say that, from what you have told, we are puzzled by Benjamin's behavior in the sense that on the one hand, we cannot realistically pretend that if Benjamin has returned to school there isn't a change, if Benjamin has started to wash himself there isn't a change, hence we cannot deny its existence. However, from the things you have told us we cannot find any connection that might explain this change.

What we mean is that, all things considered, the conditions existing one and two months ago which explained Benjamin's symptom haven't from what you have told us, substantially changed.

Hence, from our point of view, we feel that this change is totally fortuitous, in other words, it did not come about as a result of our intervention.

We might compare your situation to when a person takes some medicines, and recovers even before they have begun to take effect. Since we consider your situation identical to this, we have decided to fix another appointment, although I think things are really the way you say they are, namely, that they have and currently are changing, but because, as I said, we think this change is fortuitous, not determined by us.

This does not mean, however, that this change is not a permanent one, but at this time, frankly, we are not able to connect with our meetings. Consequently, we thought we might see each other again in two or three months, so that, if this change were to remain, we would have more elements to go on.

SIXTH SESSION: VERIFICATION AND THE CLOSURE OF THERAPY

The sixth session took place three months after the fifth one, exactly one year from the beginning of therapy. For the third time, the parents came together and told of many new developments in the family's life. Since the grandparents now need constant care, meaning by Joan, quite often after dinner they leave their children home alone (unthinkable just a few months before) to go visit their parents. In addition, Mr. Osburm finally decided to move into a single-family home which belonged to his wife (until now, he had always refused saying that "it isn't really mine"); and he also expects a bright future ahead with respect to his work, having just been promoted to another department. His wife continues to be satisfied with her job in her in-laws' store, who are slowly handing over all responsibilities to her.

The problems for which therapy had been requested have now been surmounted. David alone seems to be having a few problems adjusting to junior high. Once again, the parents blame each other; Mrs. Osburm, in particular, is described as impulsive, unpredictable, and jealous by her husband. Within the couple, there still are dark spots and reciprocal disconfirmations, but they don't seem to be as serious as in the preceding sessions.

At this time, the therapists decide the time has come to end the therapy. They tell Mr. and Mrs. Osburm that the doubts left over by the preceding session have been erased, but that their situation is like that of a patient who has just been operated upon: After the operation, he feels fine, but the scar that remains, every once in a while, especially when seasons change, starts to hurt; but since the cause is known, one should not be alarmed. Hence, in their case, the problem has been resolved. But this does not mean that in the future there won't be scars that are impossible to eliminate, and that once in a while might cause a little pain.

CONCLUSIONS

In narrating this case we have come across a family with a problem: the presence of "strange" behaviors, let us call them symptoms, in one of its members; the family had requested that the therapists cure the patient of these symptoms. What did the therapists do? First of all, they proposed to define the problem another way, namely as a problem resulting from the failure of the parental couple to define themselves as such with respect to their children. This hypothesis was gradually introduced in the family system's world view through particular conduct techniques and a few postsession interventions, because at the beginning of the therapy such a world view would not have been accepted. As a result, the symptom, after an initial worsening, disappeared altogether and even the familial modes of communication were modified (the biggest change, the one with respect to the premises, may only be inferred from what the parents said in the sixth session). At that time, therapy was terminated.

Through our first-hand experience, we may say that the hypothesis formulated by the therapeutic team on the function of the symptom and, more generally, on the family pattern, was useful. Its usefulness must be measured on the basis of the final outcome: The symptom has disappeared.

Let us study these observations more closely.

This family was self-described as pathologic; the therapists then identified a mode of communication based on reciprocal disconfirmations that, according to statistics, might give rise maybe in ten years, when the children will want to leave home, to new pathologies. A question thus arises that even at the closing of the therapy had been cause for heavy discussion among the therapeutic team. The discussion centered around the question: Is the disappearance of the symptom a sufficient parameter for the therapist to feel authorized to end the therapy? Or does the persistence of a pattern, which in his or her opinion is inadequate, justify the choice to continue?

Each time a case is to be closed, these problems inevitably arise. In this case they were particularly pressing: In the sixth session, the parents appeared still to be very involved (maybe as they never had been before), their problems had been barely touched upon, and so they were strongly tempted to continue the therapeutic relationship. The motive that finally prevailed on them to end the therapy was consistent with the professional attitude they had assumed; the aim on which the therapeutic contract had been stipulated, had been reached, the initial request had been satisfied, and to continue would have required a redefinition of the relationship on a totally different basis.

Clinicians cannot ignore their limits; only thus will they be able to avoid tasks that are not in their competence and avoid making choices that might contrast with their own world view. The problem can be summed up into one choice with two different premises. One can either cradle the idea of building heaven on earth, by changing the people and their families (for some, however, this paradise might become a living inferno); or one may think more modestly of aiding those who seek help—accepting their definition of "health" and "happiness"—without pretending to make them fit into a ready-made model.

REFERENCES

Andolfi, M. (1979). *Family Therapy: An Interactional Approach.* New York: Plenum.

Bandler, R., and Grinder, J. (1975). *The Structure of Magic.* Palo Alto: Science and Behavior Books.

Bateson, G. (1935). Culture contact and schismogenesis. *Man* 35:178–183. Also in *Steps to an Ecology of Mind,* pp. 61–72. New York: Ballantine.

_____ (1964). The logical categories of learning and communication. In *Steps to an Ecology of Mind,* pp. 279–308. New York: Ballantine.

_____ (1969). Double bind. In *Steps to an Ecology of Mind,* pp. 271–278. New York: Ballantine.

_____ (1970). Form, substance, and difference. *General Semantics Bulletin,* vol. 37. Paper presented at the 19th Annual Alfred Korzybski Memorial Lecture, New York, January 9. Also in *Steps to an Ecology of Mind,* pp. 448–465. New York: Ballantine.

———— (1971). The cybernetics of "self": a theory of alcoholism. *Psychiatry* 34:18. Also in *Steps to an Ecology of Mind*, pp. 309–337. New York: Ballantine.

———— (1972). *Steps to an Ecology of Mind*. New York: Ballantine.

———— (1979). *Mind and Nature: A Necessary Unity*. New York: Dutton.

Bateson, G., Jackson, D. D., Haley, J., and Weakland, J. H. (1956). Toward a theory of schizophrenia. *Behavioral Science* 1:251–264. Also in *Steps to an Ecology of Mind*, pp. 201–227. New York: Ballantine.

Bertalanffy, L. von. (1967). *Robots, Men, and Minds*. New York: Braziller.

———— (1969). *General System Theory*. New York: Braziller.

Buckley, W. (1967). *Sociology and Modern System Theory*. Englewood Cliffs, N.J.: Prentice-Hall.

———— (1968). *Modern Systems Research for the Behavioral Scientist*. Chicago: Aldine.

Dell, P. (1980a). The Hopi family therapist and the Aristotelian parents. *Journal of Marital and Family Therapy* 6:123–130.

———— (1980b). Researching the family theories of schizophrenia: an exercise in epistemological confusion. *Family Process* 18:321–335.

———— (1981a). More thoughts on paradox: rejoinder by Dell. *Family Process* 20:47–51.

———— (1981b). Some irreverent thoughts on paradox. *Family Process* 20:37–41.

———— (1982). Beyond homeostasis: toward a concept of coherence. *Family Process* 21:21–42.

Elkaim, M. (1981). Non equilibrium, chance and change in family therapy. *Journal of Marital and Family Therapy* 7:291–297.

Foerster, H. von. (1962). *Principles of Self Organization*. New York: Pergamon.

Gray, W., Duhl, F. J., and Rizzo, N. D., eds. (1969). *General Systems Theory and Psychiatry*. Boston: Little, Brown.

Haire, M., ed. (1959). *Modern Organization Theory*. New York: Wiley.

Haley, J. (1963). *Strategies of Psychotherapy.* New York: Grune & Stratton.

_____ (1969). Toward a theory of pathological systems. In *Family Therapy and Disturbed Families.* Palo Alto: Science and Behavior Books.

_____ (1971). *Changing Families: A Family Therapy Reader.* New York: Grune and Stratton.

_____ (1973). *Uncommon Therapy: The Psychiatric Techniques of Milton H. Erickson, M.D.* New York: W. W. Norton.

_____ (1976). *Problem Solving Therapy.* San Francisco: Jossey-Bass.

Haley, J., and Hoffman, L. (1968). *Techniques of Family Therapy.* New York: Basic Books.

Hall, A. D., and Fagen, R. E. (1956). Definition of system. *General Systems* 1:18.

Harrè, R., and Secord, P. F. (1972). *The Explanation of Social Behaviour.* Oxford: Basil Blackwell.

Hesse, M. B. (1966). *Models and Analogies in Science.* Notre Dame: University of Notre Dame Press.

Hoffman, L. (1971). Deviation-amplifying processes in natural groups. In *Changing Families: A Family Therapy Reader.* New York: Grune & Stratton.

_____ (1981). *Foundations of Family Therapy.* New York: Basic Books.

Jackson, D. D. (1957). The question of family homeostasis. *The Psychiatric Quarterly Supplement* 31:79–90.

_____ (1965a). Family rules: marital quid pro quo. *Archives of General Psychiatry* 12:589–594.

_____ (1965b). The study of the family. *Family Process* 4:1–20.

Jackson, D. D., and Weakland, J. H. (1961). Conjoint family therapy: some considerations on theory, technique, and results. *Psychiatry* 24 (Suppl.):30–45.

Keeney, B. P. (1979). Ecosystemic epistemology: an alternate paradigm for diagnosis. *Family Process* 18:117–129.

_____ (1982). What is an epistemology of family therapy? *Family Process* 21:153–168.

Keeney, B. P., and Ross, J. M. (1985). *Mind in Therapy: Constructing Systemic Family Therapies.* New York: Basic Books.

Kuhn, T. S. (1962). *The Structure of Scientific Revolutions.* Chicago: University of Chicago Press.

MacKinnon, L. (1983). Contrasting strategic and Milan therapies. *Family Process* 22:425–438.

Miller, J. G. (1965a). Living systems: basic concepts. *Behavioral Sciences* 10:193–237.

―――― (1965b). Living systems: structure and process. *Behavioral Sciences* 10:337–379.

―――― (1965c). Living systems: cross-level hypotheses. *Behavioral Sciences* 10:380–411.

Morris, C. (1955). *International Encyclopedia of Unified Science.* Chicago: University of Chicago Press.

Penn, P. (1982). Circular questioning. *Family Process* 21: 267–280.

Prigogine, I., and Stengers, I. (1979). *La Nouvelle Alliance: Metamorphose de la Science.* Paris: Gallimard.

Ricci, C., and Selvini Palazzoli, M. (1984). Interaction, complexity, and communication. *Family Process* 23:169–176.

Ruesch, J., and Bateson, G. (1951). *Communication: The Social Matrix of Psychiatry.* New York: W. W. Norton.

Selvini Palazzoli, M. (1970). Contesto e metacontesto nella psicoterapia della famiglia. *Archivio di Psicologia, Neurologia e Psichiatria* 31:203–211.

―――― (1978a). *Self-Starvation.* New York: Jason Aronson.

―――― (1978b). Terapia della famiglia a transazione schizofrenica. l controlle terapeutico del sovrasistema famiglia-terapisti. *Terapia Familiare* 3:67–74.

―――― (1981). Comments on Dell's paper. *Family Process* 10:44–45.

―――― (1984). Review of "Aesthetics of Change" by Bradford Keeney. *Family Process* 23:282–284.

Selvini Palazzoli, M., Boscolo, L., Cecchin, G., and Prata, G. (1977a). Family rituals: a powerful tool in family therapy. *Family Process* 16:445–453.

―――― (1977b). La prima seduta di una terapia familiare sistemica. *Terapia Familiare* 2:5–13.

―――― (1978). *Paradox and Counterparadox.* New York: Jason Aronson.

_____ (1980a). Hypothesizing-circularity-neutrality. *Family Process* 19:3–12.

_____ (1980b). The problem of the referring person. *Journal of Marital and Family Therapy* 6:3–9.

_____ (1983). *Behind the Scenes of the Organization*. New York: Pantheon Books.

Sluzki, C. E. (1975). The coalitionary process in initiating family therapy. *Family Process* 14:67–77.

Sluzki, C. E., and Beavin, J. (1965). Symmetry and complementarity. In *The Interactional View*. New York: W. W. Norton.

Sluzki, C. E., Beavin, J., Tarnopolski, A., and Veron, E. (1967). Transactional disqualifications. In *The Interactional View*. New York: W. W. Norton.

Sluzki, C. E., and Ransom, D. C. (1976). *Double Bind: The Foundation of the Communicational Approach to the Family*. New York: Grune and Stratton.

Speer, D. C. (1970). Family systems: morphostasis and morphogenesis, or "is homeostasis enough?" *Family Process* 9:259–278.

Viaro, M., and Leonardi, P. (1983). Getting and giving information: analysis of a family-interview strategy. *Family Process* 22:27–42.

Vogel, E. F., and Bell, N. W. (1960). The emotionally disturbed child as the family scapegoat. In *A Modern Introduction to the Family*, ed. E. F. Vogel and N. W. Bell, pp. 412–427. New York: The Free Press.

Watzlawick, P. (1976). *"How Real Is Real?* New York: Vintage Books.

_____ (1977). *Die Möglichkeit des Andersseins: Zur Technik der Therapeutischen Kommunikation*. Bern: Hans Huber.

Watzlawick, P., Beavin, J. H., and Jackson, D. D. (1967). *Pragmatics of Human Communication: A Study of Interactional Patterns, Pathologies and Paradoxes*. New York: W. W. Norton.

Watzlawick, P., and Weakland, J. H., eds. (1977). *The Interactional View*. New York: W. W. Norton.

Watzlawick, P., Weakland, J. H., and Fisch, R. (1974). *Change: Principles of Problem Formation and Problem Resolution*. New York: W. W. Norton.

Weakland, J. H. (1960). The "double bind" hypothesis of schizophrenia and three-party interaction. In *The Etiology of Schizophrenia*. New York: Basic Books.

Weakland, J. H., Fisch, R., Watzlawick, P., and Bodin, A. M. (1974). Brief therapy: focused problem resolution. *Family Process* 13:141–168.

Weeks, G. R., and L'Abate, J. (1982). *Paradoxical Psychotherapy: Theory and Practice with Individuals, Couples and Families*. New York: Brunner/Mazel.

Wiener, N. (1965). *Cybernetics, or Control and Communication in the Animal and the Machine*. Cambridge: MIT Press.

Wittgenstein, L. (1956). *Bemerkungen über die Grundlagen der Mathematik*. Oxford: Blackwell Scientific.

INDEX